Candle for Poland:
469 Days of
Solidarity

Stokvis Studies in Historical Chronology & Thought
Number Two
ISSN 0270-5338

Leszek Szymański
With an Introduction by Dr. Jeffrey M. Elliot

R. Reginald

The Borgo Press

San Bernardino, California
MCMLXXXII

For Robert Reginald—
in friendship

Library of Congress Cataloging in Publication Data:

Szymanski, Leszek, 1933-
  Candle for Poland.

  (Stokvis studies in historical chronology and thought ; no. 2)
  Bibliography: p. 119.
  1. NSZZ "Solidarnosc" (Labor organization).   2. Trade-unions—
Poland—Political activity. I. Title. II. Series.
HD8537.N783S98   322'.2'09438   82-1231
ISBN 0-89370-166-1 (cloth, $10.95)   AACR2
ISBN 0-89370-266-8 (paper, $4.95)

Edited by R. Reginald. Produced, designed, and published by R. Reginald and Mary A. Burgess, The Borgo Press, P.O. Box 2845, San Bernardino, CA 92406 USA. Printed in the United States of America by Victory Press, San Bernardino, CA. Binding by California Zip Bindery,
San Bernardino, CA. Cover and title page design by Michael Pastucha.

First Edition————June, 1982

Contents

Introduction

In a speech to the CPSU Congress in February, 1981, Soviet President Leonid Brezhnev enunciated his nation's position on the tragic events taking place in Poland today. He said, in part: "In fraternal Poland . . . the enemies of socialism, with the support of outside forces, are creating anarchy and endeavoring to turn the development of events into a counterrevolutionary channel . . . . A threat to the foundations of the socialist state has arisen . . . . We will stand up for socialist Poland, fraternal Poland, and will not leave her in the lurch . . . . Communists have always boldly met the attacks of the adversary and won out. This is how it was and how it will be, and let not one person have any doubt about our common determination to secure our interests and defend the peoples' socialist gains."

In a carefully worded speech, Secretary of State Alexander Haig articulated the position of the United States, declaring: "After eighteen months, Solidarity has been violently suppressed. December 13, 1981 began the descent for Poland and for the world. The Communist authorities, mocking their own propaganda, threw the armed machinery of the state against the worker. The results are clear for all to see. Instead of dignity, there is degradation. Instead of truth, there is violation of conscience. Instead of freedom, there is fear."

In this war of words, who is correct? Did Solidarity itself, as the Soviets contend, bring about its own suppression through excesses that endangered Poland's entire economy? Is it true, as the Soviets maintain, that they did not intervene in Poland and have had nothing to do with the suppression of Solidarity? Does General Jaruzelski's regime, as the Soviets argue, deserve support because the "state of war" in Poland is the act of Polish nationalists, concerned that something worse will happen unless Communist-style law and order are established? Is it the case, as the Soviets insist, that Poland's misfortunes are none of America's business, that we have no right to judge the situation nor influence it?

The present volume, *Candle for Poland*, seeks to answer these and other questions. It does so, in my judgment, in an intelligent, thoughtful, and objective manner. In analyzing the current situation through December 1981, Dr. Szymanski takes a critical look at recent events in Poland, in a way that will shed new light on the emergence of Solidarity and the role that it has played and will continue to play in that struggle. He also brings together for the first time the basic documents necessary for any serious study of the problem; many of these have been translated from the original Polish texts.

Most Americans understand, only too clearly, that what happens in Poland will have far-reaching consequences not only for that distant country, but for the United States and the rest of the world. Americans, however, have a special interest in the events taking place in Poland today. This is true not only because there are many Americans of Polish descent in this country—as well as friends and neighbors who empathize with their plight—but because the future of Poland is inextricably linked to the struggle for freedom itself. As President Reagan has asserted: "Make no mistake. The tragic events in the East have a profound meaning for us in the West. Our progress, despite all of our faults, is a striking rebuke to the Soviet system. After all, what the Polish people sought was not more than we take for granted, as natural to us as the air we breathe . . . . As the trustees of peace and freedom, it is only through our strength and resolve, our passion for the defense of our liberties, that we earn the right to say to the Polish people: The day will dawn after the terror of the night."

Clearly, all the threads of a nation's domestic and foreign policy are intimately interwoven. However, only when these threads are interwoven do they attain the strength of fabric, and only when we the weavers share a common vision does the fabric become a tapestry. America's policy toward Poland, both now and in the future, must, I think, reflect our country's historic commitment to the ideals of freedom and justice. We must stand today, as our forebears did centuries ago, with those who prize the dignity of man and the search for freedom.

The task of resolving the present crisis in Poland is, as the author suggests, not only extraordinarily complex, but extremely urgent. It involves discarding many old precepts and evolving radical new ones. As Rollo May, the world-renowned psychiatrist, puts it, "the old ideas are dying and the new ones haven't yet been born." Dr. Szymanski, both in his summary and analysis, provides us with the insights and tools necessary to tackle these problems with intelligence, understanding, and inventiveness.

This period of crisis, however, has two faces. The ancient Chinese were well aware of this duality, for their character for "crisis" is made up of two characters; one means danger, the other opportunity. The danger is that our courage will fail, that we will abandon our commitment to the extension of freedom, as well as those for whom it is but a far-off dream. *Candle for Poland* serves to remind us of what can happen when freedom is extinguished; when a people are denied their birthright and are forced to serve an oppressive master. The present volume seeks to enhance our understanding of the problems which plague Poland, both past and present, but it also serves to remind us of our own time-honored commitment to the ideals of freedom and justice. At stake is not only the freedom of the Poles, but freedom, itself.

The attainment of true freedom is dependent upon our ability (meaning the principle involved, both directly and indirectly) to create conditions which will allow freedom to take root and grow. I use the phrase— "take root and grow"—advisedly, for freedom is like a plant in that it needs a balanced environment to grow and mature. It cannot develop in acid soil and in conditions of total darkness. We must recognize, as the author points out, that the true freedom the Polish people desire can only grow in a balanced fertile soil. This soil must contain within its humus a reasonable degree of political, social, and economic democracy, if freedom is to take root and prosper. These three aspects of society— the political, the social, and the economic—are inseparable, and hence there can be no political democracy unless there is also social and economic democracy. It is this lesson, above all others, which must be learned.

It is to be hoped that Secretary Haig is correct when he proclaimed: "Poland has not perished. Poland cannot perish. The exponents of Marxism-Leninism in Warsaw or Moscow, who pride themselves on knowledge of the laws of history, have ignored this basic truth. The sight of a peaceful people seeking peaceful change has terrified them. But the actions of these fearful men will not deprive the Poles of their faith, their courage, or their sacred dreams. Change will come. Hope will be reborn. And Poland will truly be Poland again."

Dr. Jeffrey M. Elliot
Durham, North Carolina
April, 1982

Chapter 1

Struggle for Bread and Freedom:
The Magna Carta in the Soviet Empire

When in August, 1980 the news about the historic Gdansk Accord reached the West, the name of the new trade union, Solidarity ("Solidarnosc" in Polish), was practically unknown; nor was the significance of the wave of Polish strikes which had culminated on the Baltic coast yet comprehensible.

The Polish press euphemistically referred to the strikes as "work stoppages." Lech Walesa's name was not yet mentioned (in Polish, the word *"walesa"* has some curious connotations, meaning something between a wanderer and a tramp). Even much later, some people present at the heart of the events did not realize what was happening. An eyewitness, a white collar worker, writes:

> We did not know that on Thursday a big strike was going to happen...We had heard on the internal radio that at 4 p.m. one more meeting would take place between the management and the strike committee...Later on an occupation strike was announced. Leaving home, I and many of my colleagues were not prepared for any longer stay at work. The form of strike—sit-in—surprised us....The strike committee assured us that anyone who wanted to could leave the shipyard. But despite that the Workers' Guard made troubles....I thought I saw the people who wanted to leave being pushed around....Someone spit at their feet. I heard abuses. In my presence only three persons left the shipyard (Biblioteka Pomostu, *Polski Sierpien 1980* [New York: Biblioteka Pomostu, 1981], p. 247).

But the troubles in Poland were brewing a long time before Walesa climbed the Lenin Shipyard fence to join the strikers and Solidarity, becoming in the process a folk hero both in Poland and abroad; and before a half-literate female worker, Anna Walentynowicz, became, almost, a Polish Jeanne d'Arc.

In 1945, the Western allies, tired by war, hoping for a new world order depending on the Big Three powers, offered Poland to Russia as a token of good will. The only conditions were that some of the friendly "London Poles" would be coopted into the government set up by the Russians, and that there would be "free elections." Almost immediately, England and the U.S. withdrew recognition from the Polish Government in exile. The Soviet Union, of course, had already recognized its own creation, the Lublin Committee, long before. Poland was thus left morally and physically to its own devices, under effective control of the Soviets. A Stalinist reign of terror was soon introduced, and the so-called free elections remained an unrealized part of Roosevelt's Yalta dreams. The precursor of Solidarity, the Polish Peasant Party, the only organized opposition to the new regime, was ruthlessly crushed [The Polish Peasant Party (PSL) combined elements of a political party with characteristics of a mass movement, uniting, in spite of its name, intellectuals, workers, and peasants in joint opposition to the Soviet-controlled administration].

After Stalin's death in 1953, the apparatus of terror was partially dismantled, which led to the so-called Polish October Revolution of 1956. This first public sign of disenchantment with the Soviets was presaged by a workers' revolt in Poznan over food prices. Wladyslaw Gomulka, a stubborn communist who had been accused by Stalin of Titoism, was returned to power, and quickly moved the country into the orthodox fold. He was successful in introducing higher meat prices in 1959, but his next attempt to raise the cost of staple food items led to a workers' rebellion on the Baltic Coast in 1970, and Gomulka's subsequent fall.

Gomulka's successor, Edward Gierek, increased wages while simultaneously raising food prices; but some of the women workers started angry demonstrations against the regime, forcing him to rescind the price hikes while leaving in place the salary adjustments. Gierek then promulgated an ambitious expansion of heavy industry, hoping to earn money for Poland in good capitalistic fashion by trading with hard currency countries in the West. The Western bankers willingly lent the money, and Gierek's "economic miracle" was launched. Unfortunately, the triple combination of mismanagement, bad planning, and plain ignorance of western markets doomed the Polish export drive to failure. Meanwhile, wages rose 40% from 1970 to 1975, and imports of grain and fodder increased fourfold. Meat consumption went from 132 pounds per capita in 1970 to 154 in 1980. The state was subsidizing this artificial price structure to such an extent that it absorbed about one-third of the national budget.

When in 1973 and 1974 OPEC took on the global economic system as it was then constituted, Poland was one of the major casualties, its exports suffering even further. Gierek temporarily solved the problem by borrowing more money to pay Poland's debts, in a continuously spiraling downward cycle. The country's western debts jumped from $4.8 billion in 1974 to about $25 billion in 1981. The situation further deteriorated due to lack of spare parts and a series of bad harvests.

Gierek had eventually been forced by his economic problems to increase prices in 1976, but was immediately faced with riots at the Ursus Tractor Factory near Warsaw, and at the town of Radom. The disturbances were brutally put down, and officially ascribed to "hooligans" and the ever-present "imperialistic agents." During this period, civil liberties and intellectual freedom began gradually to grow. Thus, Jacek Kuron and others were able to form the semi-legal Committee for Social Defense (KOR), ostensibly to help the workers arrested in Ursus and Radom. In fact, the Committee became a center of the dissent, and forged the first links between the intellectuals and the working class.

The first illegal free trade unions were formed in Radom in 1977, and in the mining district of Silesia and on the Baltic Coast in 1978. Two clandestine journals of great influence appeared: *Robotnik* (*Worker*) and *Placowka* (*The Outpost*). In the summer of 1979, *Robotnik* printed a "Charter of Workers' Rights," which demanded the right to strike, and the formation of the independent trade unions. Also in that year, the Polish Pope, Jan Pawel or John Paul II, visited his homeland for the first time after his election in 1978, and was greeted by millions of people who were now beginning to realize their social and numerical strength.

This, briefly, is the background of the events leading up to the Solidarity movement, a phenomenon of tremendous symbolic importance to the people of Eastern Europe. For the first time in a communist state, the threat of a workers' uprising has drastically changed the balance of power between the military and the Party, leading to the creation of the only communist military regime in Europe, and making Poland totally dependent on the Soviet Union. But Solidarity also inspired great hope for the Polish people, and for all the peoples of Eastern Europe; it also served to demonstrate, unfortunately, just how difficult it is to secure basic intellectual freedoms under a communist-governed state, and just how easy it is to lose them again. The crisis began, as usual, with discontent over government-imposed cost increases.

On July 2, 1980 the Government announced an approximately hundred-percent rise in various meat prices. In response, workers at the Ursus Tractor Factory, a hornets' nest of labor troubles for the government, immediately went on strike. Other labor actions followed throughout the country, combined with angry remonstrations. The KSS "KOR" offered its services to workers and intellectuals as an information center [The Komitet Samoobrony Spolecznej, "Komitet Obrony Robotnikow" (or in English the Social Self-defense Committee, Workers' Defense Committee) was an opposition group formed in

September 1976 to campaign for the release of workers imprisoned after the June 1976 strikes, which had been directed against food price increases]. In addition to striking, workmen began discussing management and production questions.

The strikes spread with the elementary force of a brush fire. The workers demanded and received pay raises in direct negotiations with management, omitting the customary Government and Party channels. In spite of the explosive situation, the First Secretary of the Polish United Workers' Party [The Polish United Workers' Party (Polska Zjednoczona Partia Robotnicza) is the official name of the Polish Communist Party, henceforth referred to as "PUWP" or the "Party"], Edward Gierek, left Warsaw for a working holiday in the Crimea. He met there with Leonid Brezhnev; the two leaders subsequently issued a communique saying they had exchanged information on the situations in their respective countries, but not specifically mentioning the labor unrest in Poland.

Meanwhile, the Polish Party's official publications had finally admitted the existence of the strikes. Once this reality had been acknowledged, always a difficult step in a communist system, the strikes were then officially interpreted as danger signals. The position of the Party was that there could not be basic changes in the Polish political and economic structure. The Government would continue with the new food prices, and increases in wages would be linked directly to productivity; however, the trade unions would be given a greater role in management than before, and the workers' justified claims would be considered.

The Party simply did not know how to deal with the situation. Jerzy Lukasiewicz, Chief of Propaganda at the Politbureau, stated that the strikes were purely economic in nature, but elements hostile to socialism had attempted to utilize them for their subversive value.

On August 14, flyers were distributed among the Lenin Shipyard workers in Gdansk requesting reinstatement of a certain worker, Anna Walentynowicz, and appealing to the workers' solidarity:

> To the workers of Gdansk Shipyard. We appeal to you as the workmates of Anna Walentynowicz. She has been working in the Shipyard since 1950. ...She has been always an exemplary employee, and a human being who reacted to every injustice, to each harm. These [characteristics] caused her decision to start activities aimed at the creation of independent trade unions. Since that time she has been discriminated against (Biblioteka Pomostu, p. 9).

Walentynowicz, claimed the flyer, had been illegally dismissed five months before, as a direct result of her labor activities. "In your own interest you should defend such people or one day you might find yourselves in their shoes" (Ibid.), continued the appeal. It was signed by the founding committee of free unions and the editorial staff of *Robot-*

nik (*Worker*), namely: Bogdan Borusewicz, Joanna Duda-Gwiazda, Andrzej Gwiazda, Jan Karandziej, Maryla Plonska, and Lech Walesa (listed in last place, a position he would not occupy for long).

In the yard itself, bills were posted demanding Walentynowicz's reinstatement, and a pay raise for workers of one thousand zlotys, with wages tied directly to inflation. There was a mass meeting at 8:00 A.M., during which the strike leaders made speeches; the director of the Lenin Shipyard made a response of his own. About 9:00 A.M. Lech Walesa suddenly appeared, using a bulldozer as an improvised podium.

Walesa announced (with rather unusual loyalty) that he still felt himself a yard laborer in spite of not having worked there for four years. [Lech Walesa was fired from his job in Gdansk Shipyard in April 1976. William F. Robinson, ed., *August 1980, The Strikes in Poland* (Munich: Radio Free Europe, 1981), p. 338]. He proposed a sit-in strike.

A strike committee was formed which requested reinstatement of Anna Walentynowicz and Lech Walesa, erection of a monument to the victims of the repressed strike on the Baltic coast in December of 1970, no retribution against the strikers, a pay raise of two thousand zlotys, and family benefits equal to those of the militia (the police) and the Security Forces.

For management, the easiest course was giving in on Walentynowicz, who was no doubt a troublemaker and sob-sister from their point of view; an automobile was sent for her. On her arrival Walentynowicz joined the Strike Committee. The local Party leader, Tadeusz Fiszbach, now appeared on the scene of the negotiations.

Management soon agreed to reinstate Walentynowicz and Walesa, as well as other victims of political repression; it promised not to persecute the strikers, and to build the memorial to the victims of 1970. The last concession had special significance, as such permits were not granted lightly, nor left to free initiative; otherwise, one would expect thousands of Katyn monuments. This indicated that management had been in touch with the Central Committee of the Party in Warsaw, and had been told to take a soft line against the workers.

But the strikers were not satisfied, and the labor unrest spread to other yards in Gdansk, then to the whole metropolis of Gdansk, Gdynia, and Sopot (called the Tri-Cities); even city transit stopped. The Government, in retribution, cut off telephone and telex communications. The Tri-Cities were isolated from the rest of the country, as Poznan had been in 1956.

By August 15, Gierek (probably remembering the fate of his predecessor, comrade "Wieslaw" Wladyslaw Gomulka) was starting to worry. He interrupted his Crimean feriae and returned to Warsaw. The Prime Minister, Edward Babiuch, made a televised speech in which he was conciliatory but stern: meat prices, he said, would remain at the present level until the fall of 1981. He also indicated that there was no miracle cure for the economy, that endless pay raises would just worsen the situation; Poland had lived too long on its credit, consistently consuming more than it produced. The day before, the Warsaw Party paper, *Trybuna Ludu (People's Tribune)*, had put the matter succinctly in a headline: "Wallets may swallow but queues for food will get longer" (*Trybuna Ludu* [Warsaw], 14 August 1980, p. 1).

Babiuch's speech was also significant in its allusion to the Soviet Union's possible intervention in the situation; he ended with an appeal for workers to return to work.

On the same day, TASS, the Soviet news agency, announced routine maneuvers of the Warsaw Pact armies in East Germany and the Baltic areas (i.e., on the Polish frontiers).

The Catholic Church reacted too. Stefan Cardinal Wyszynski delivered a sermon on Jasna Gora in Czestochowa [Czestochowa is a symbolic place to the Poles. The Palulins' Monastery, situated atop Bright Mountain (Jasna Gora), played a crucial role in the war with the Swedes (1655). The siege of Czestochowa is the climatic point of an epopoeiac novel by Henryk Sienkiewicz. The very name, Czestochowa, has a patriotic association for the average Pole. The picture of the Black Madonna is famous for its miracles and is a major goal for pilgrimages. Czestochowa was successfully defended against the Russians by the later American patriot Kazimierz Pulaski in 1770]. Bread, he said, was the property of the entire nation, and Poles were asking for it in a tactful and dignified manner. The old man, a stalwart anti-communist and ex-opponent of Gomulka, prayed for freedom and for the right of self-determination.

Meanwhile, the Lenin Shipyard in Gdansk took on the appearance of a Catholic fortress besieged by Pagan Tartars or Turks, or perhaps Protestant Swedes [all traditional enemies and invaders of Poland].

Holy pictures were displayed on fences and walls, among the most prominent being those of the Virgin Mary, the Queen of the Polish Crown, and ex-cardinal Karol Wojtyla (now Pope John Paul II), accompanied by the Polish national colors of white and red, and the national coat of arms (the white eagle). The Workers' Guard, dressed in overalls with white/red bands and hard hats, looked strangely militaristic, reminding one of the Warsaw insurrectionists of 1944.

An open-air Mass authorized by Gdansk Bishop Lech Kaczmarek was celebrated by three priests; Kaczmarek also sent the strike committee medals of the Pope. About five thousand strikers piously attended the services inside, and a crowd of about two thousand worshipped outside the gate. After the Mass, a huge cross was erected at Gate Number Two, the place where the workers had been killed in 1970. Another Mass, with an equally impressive attendance, took place at the Gdynia Shipyard.

The Interfactory Strike Committee (Miedzyzakladowy Komitet Strajkowy, or MKS) was established to coordinate the strikes, being composed of representatives from the Lenin Shipyard and other striking establishments.

On the Government's side, the Deputy Prime Minister, Tadeusz Pyka, was nominated the head of a special commission to examine the Gdansk crisis. A local member of that commission, party dignitary Tadeusz Fiszbach, appealed over the local television for peace and a return to work.

The workers had nearly returned to their jobs when, on the previous day, the Lenin Shipyard management had yielded on the last point of the original demands by the strikers (i.e., pay increases). Lech Walesa declared the strike ended. When it appeared, however, that the bargaining position of the other striking units would weaken, the strike was renewed. New postulates were put forward, such as freedom of speech and information, free trade unions, and release of political prisoners (probably on the advice of the dissidents present at the strike center from the beginning). Thus, the strikers' demands ceased to have a local and economic character, and became instead an essential problem for the communist system.

Among the strikers' demands, but not included on the national list, was a request for prohibition of alcoholic beverages. This was granted locally; but if it had remained on the national agenda, it would no doubt have cut short the strikers' popularity.

On Monday, August 18, 1980, the workers who had thought the strike was finished and had returned to work were suddenly informed that the strike was very much alive and well in Gdansk.

The situation was serious. Edward Gierek, after a Politbureau meeting, made a national broadcast on television and radio. His speech was highly conciliatory: national economic priorities would be shifted to the supply side of the market, he said, with meat imports increased, wages and various allowances boosted, and the official trade unions reformed. But no challenge to the basic socialist foundation of the state would be tolerated.

The speech had no effect whatever. In the Gdansk Shipyard, few even bothered to listen. The strikes spread along the entire Baltic shore and then burst into other parts of Poland. The strikers adopted the national colors, emblem, and anthem as their symbols. Now, the Chairman of the State Council, Henryk Jablonski, and a member of the Politbureau, Security boss Stanislaw Kania, arrived in Gdansk. Pyka, the head of the Government negotiating team, was replaced by another Deputy Prime Minister, Mieczyslaw Jagielski. Jagielski was considered an expert in bargaining due to his success in the Lublin strikes a month previously. Reluctantly, the Government Commission agreed to talk directly with the Interfactory Strike Committee instead of negotiating with the individual enterprises.

On August 23, the Interfactory Strike Committee (ISC-MKS) placed its celebrated twenty-one points before Jagielski, comparatively much bolder demands than those presented by the barons to King John in 1214. [These demands were handed to Jagielski on August 23rd (Radio Free Europe). According to *Tygodnik Solidarnosc* (Warsaw), August 21, 1980, the demands were formulated on August 16. Some of the intellectuals present were Bogdan Borusewicz, Andrzej Gwiazda and his wife Joanna, and Bogdan Lis. On August 21, Lech Badkowski and Wojciech Gruszecki were coopted to the Praesidium of the ISC (MKS). The "official" intellectual experts arrived in Gdansk on August 25. Thus, the precise authorship of this "constitution" and the relationship to and influence of the intellectuals and dissidents is not clear to me. On August 18, the membership of the ISC Praesidium included: Lech Walesa, Joanna Duda-Gwiazda, Bogdan Lis, Anna Walentynowicz, Florian Wisniewski, Lech Jendruszewski, Stefan Izdebski, Henryka Krzywonos, Tadeusz Stanny, Stefan Lewandowski, Lech Sobieszek, Jozef Przybylski, Zdzislaw Kobylinski, Andrzej Gwiazda, Jerzy Sikorski, Jerzy Kmiecik, Andrzej Kolodziej. Borusewicz had no official role.]

On August 25, the fourth Plenum of PUWP (Polish United Workers' Party, PZPR) met, and a major shake-up of the Party leadership and Government followed. Prime Minister Babiuch was sacked; he was replaced by Jozef Pinkowski. The following notables were eased out of the Politbureau: Jerzy Lukasiewicz (the head of the CC's Ideological-Educational Department), Jan Szydlak (official trade union boss), Tadeusz Wrzaszczyk (Chairman of the Planning Commission), and Zdzislaw Zandarowski. The changes in government (except for the removal of Maciej Szczepanski, the television and radio tsar) were not as important as the changes in the Politbureau, especially the return of Stefan Olszowski and Tadeusz Grabski. Both men had previously dared to criticize Gierek and had then been kicked out of the Politbureau; now they were back in positions of power.

The main speech to the Plenum was made by Kania. Comrade Gierek did address the assembly, but indulged mainly in self-criticism, a highly dangerous exercise for a party leader. He acknowledged the need for a radical change in the Party and Government policies, and apologized to those whose advice, in the past, he had not heeded. Gierek rejected the idea of free unions but promised a democratic procedure for electing union officials, that is, a secret ballot and unlimited number of candidates.

So the sacrifice was made. Babiuch, who was in office only four months, served as a surrogate Gierek. Lukasiewicz was blamed by his colleagues for the ideological mess. Pyka was not good enough at negotiations with Solidarity. Szydlak was responsible for the trade unions, the most obvious person to be blamed for the Party's and the nation's troubles. Wrzaszczyk was responsible for planning, while Szczepanski, called "Bloody Maciek," had political enemies who were happy to use the widespread rage resulting from his restrictive information policies during the critical period of the Gdansk events to settle old accounts.

While these changes were taking place, the Interfactory Strike Committee decided not to talk with the Government Commission unless communications with the rest of the country were restored. The Government complied, and the talks grudgingly resumed while the strikes continued throughout Poland. The strikers in each area were presenting their own individual lists of demands, sometimes as many as forty in the case of Nowa Huta, a steel combine near Krakow. The Government retaliated with some arrests, and in its press organs accused the KOR and an emigre publishing house, *Kultura*, of exploiting the workers' justified demands for subversive political purposes. TASS expressed the Russians' fear of the anti-socialist elements rampant in Poland. On August 31, the Government and the Gdansk strikers signed a final agreement. The Government conceded to all twenty-one points:

1. Acceptance of free trade unions independent of the Communist Party and of state enterprises, in accordance with convention No. 87 of the International Labor Organization, concerning the right to form free trade unions, which was ratified by the Communist Government of Poland.
2. A guarantee of the right to strike and of the security of strikers and those aiding them.
3. Compliance with the constitutional guarantee of freedom of speech, the press, and publication, including freedom of independent publishers, and the availability of the mass media to representatives of all faiths.
4. (a) a return of former rights to people dismissed from work after the 1970 and 1976 strikes, and to students expelled from school because of their views.
   (b) the release of all political prisoners, among them Edmund Zadrozynski, Jan Kozlowski, and Marek Kozlowski.
   (c) a halt to repression of individuals because of personal convictions.
5. Availability to the mass media of information about the formation of the Interfactory Strike Committee and publication of its demands.
6. The undertaking of actions aimed at bringing the country out of its crisis situation by the following means:
   (a) making public complete information about the socio-economic situation.
   (b) enabling all sectors and social classes to take part in discussions on the reform program.
7. Compensation for all workers taking part in the strike for the period of the strike, with vacation pay from the Central Council of Trade Unions.
8. An increase in the base pay of each worker by 2,000 zlotys a month as compensation for the recent rise in prices.
9. Guaranteed automatic increases in pay based on increases in prices and the decline in real income.
10. A full supply of food products for the domestic market, with exports limited to surpluses.
11. The abolition of "commercial" prices and of other sales for hard currency in special shops.

12. The selection of management personnel on the basis of qualifications, not party membership. Privileges of the secret police, regular police, and the Party apparatus to be eliminated by equalizing family subsidies, abolishing special stores, etc.

13. The introduction of food coupons for meat and meat products during the period in which the economy is brought back under control.

14. Reduction in the retirement age for women to 50 and for men to 55, or after 30 years' employment in Poland for women and 35 years' for men, regardless of age.

15. Conformity of old-age pensions and annuities to what has actually been paid in.

16. Improvements in the health service to insure full medical care for all workers.

17. Assurances of a reasonable number of day-care centers and kindergartens for the children of working mothers.

18. Paid maternity leave for three years.

19. A decrease in the waiting period for apartments.

20. An increase in the commuter's allowance to 100 zlotys from 40, with a supplemental benefit on separation.

21. A day of rest on Saturday. Workers in the brigade system or round-the-clock jobs are to be compensated for the loss of free Saturdays with increased leave or other paid time off (Oliver MacDonald, ed., *The Polish August* [San Francisco: Ztangi Press, 1981], p. 35).

The actual record of negotiations is not available. The partial record, published in *Polski Sierpien 1980* (Biblioteka Pomostu, p. 55), shows that there was little bargaining during the negotiations. Solidarity delegates accused the Government of various misdeeds, and Jagielski conceded, explained, or denied. The agreement represented the CC's unconditional surrender more than Jagielski's diplomacy.

After weeks of tension, underlined by the threat of Soviet invasion, it seemed that everybody accepted the solution. The truce was signed. The ceremony was shown on national television; the spirit of agreement expressed in speeches by Walesa and Jagielski came out loud and clear to the Poles, who were well versed in Aesopian metaphor. Said Walesa: ". . . I should like to thank once again Mr. Prime Minister and all the forces which did not allow the use of force to settle the matter. Indeed, we came to an agreement as Pole with Pole . . . ." (Jean Offredo, *Lech Walesa Czyli Polskie Lato* [Paris: Edicione Dominique Le Core, 1981], p. 109).

Answered Jagielski: ". . . We talked as Poles should talk with Poles . . . . There are no victors or vanquished" (Ibid., p. 111). This meant, in plain Polish, that those concerned talked as patriots, not communist servants of Moscow. For any careful student of the Gdansk Accord, it is clear that the Government (i.e., the Party) was utterly desperate to agree to such political and economic demands. From an economic point of view, granting these economic desiderata was a green light for inflation and an invitation to the country's ruin.

The Polish workers did not believe that their situation, compared to that in the West, was as bad as imagined. They had to wait years for apartments, but once they got them they paid a nominal rent. They enjoyed numerous social benefits, such as long vacations at holiday resorts arranged by the "old" trade unions, summer camps for children, subsidized lunches at workplaces, socialized medicine, and relatively easy jobs. What they missed was not so much material goods, as freedom.

In spite of Walesa's disclaimers, demands were political, national in scope and aimed at the very basis of the system; this was especially true of the request to liquidate the Party members' and Security Forces' privileges. If the Party honestly intended to keep its side of the bargain, it would at best be left in an impossible situation of being beholden to Moscow while still responsible to the people—an awkward situation, reminiscent of that of the royal governors in Colonial America.

On August 30, a different Governmental Commission signed an agreement with the strikers in Szczecin, another important Baltic port. The Szczecin agreement was less publicized because, though most of the strikers' demands were similar to those of their Gdansk comrades, the all-important Marxism semantic was different. The key phrase allowing the creation of autonomous trade unions stated: ". . . It was agreed that, if supported by the opinion of experts, autonomous trade unions may be formed which will have socialistic character in accordance with the constitution of the Polish People's Republic" [*Protokoly Porozumien Gdansk Szczecin, Jastrzebie* (Warsaw: RSW "Prasa-Ksiazka-Ruch," 1981), p. 10. I have checked this government-published text and found that it is no different than those independently printed abroad. The Polish Constitution says: "The Polish People's Republic shall be a socialistic state" (Article 1), and "The Polish United Workers' Party shall be the guiding political force of society in building socialism" (Article 2). Friendship and cooperation with the Soviet Union is assured by Article 3. *Constitution of the Polish People's Republic* (Warsaw: Krajowa Agencja Wydawnicza, 1981), p. 17].

On September 6, still another agreement was reached, this time with the striking miners in Silesia, whose actions had crippled the all-important Polish coal industry. The signing ceremony took place in Jastrzebie. The agreement confirmed the Gdansk Accord, and introduced a number of points specific to the mining industry.

On September 5, Prime Minister Jozef Pinkowski made a speech at the opening session of the Polish Parliament (*Diet Sejm*), presenting Government proposals on pay increases and controls, market supplies, and on workers' self-government. He admitted that some strikes were still continuing.

The debate which followed centered on the severe criticism of the Government, and thus, specifically, of the Party's leadership. The non-party deputy, Karol Malcuzynski, attacked the information and propaganda apparatus for suppressing any form of social dialogue, a policy which alienated citizens to such an extent that even the official data on floods were not believed! Jan Szczepanski, another non-party deputy, also criticized the censorship. Bernard Kus, of the United Peasant Party, protested against the Parliament being a rubber stamp for the Party, as did a Catholic deputy, Janusz Zablocki. Even Andrzej Zabinski, one of the CC Secretaries, who later the same day was to become a Politbureau member, inveighed against the censorship, as if not aware that it was imposed according to the Party's instructions.

Gierek's absence from the session was noted. Towards the end of the proceedings, an announcement was made about his unexpected illness. This was a very significant development, since in the communist system leaders rarely recover from this kind of illness, especially if it has been preceded by self-criticism.

Late that night the political health of Gierek worsened, and he was ousted from his post as the Party's First Secretary, being replaced by Stanislaw Kania, the "apparatchik" Head of Internal Security. Leonid Brezhnev quickly congratulated the new leader, describing him as a staunch fighter for communism and the people, and a firm supporter of the Soviet Union.

Kania, in a speech to the CC broadcast by the Media, promised to honor commitments signed with the workers. At the same time, the Government formally approved increases in wages, pensions, and family benefits. It raised the price of agricultural products paid to the peasants, and allowed the local authorities a greater measure of discretion, while making them directly responsible for economic development of their own areas.

Kania, accompanied by Jagielski, paid a visit to Gdansk. There, in a conference on the voievodship of party "aktiv," past events and the present situation were assessed. He promised that the Party would study the causes of the crisis and prevent their repetition. It would reestablish the bond with the proletariat and would promote an authentic labor movement. He alluded to future Party purges and an extraordinary Congress. He assured the "aktiv" that the Soviet Union and other socialist countries would help Poland.

The same day, the Deputy Prime Minister in charge of Polish finance, Henryk Kisiel, revealed that Poland's foreign debt now exceeded twenty billion dollars, and that the Soviet Union had given 550 million dollars credit to Poland since May, 1980.

Gierek's era had ended, but Kania's era never quite arrived. This was the Solidarity epoch. All over the country independent, self-governing trade unions were being formed. Nonetheless, the various strikes continued. The State Council passed a formal resolution which enabled the registration of new unions. A special section of the Warsaw Voievodship Court under Zdzislaw Koscielniak was responsible. Kazimierz Switon made the first application as leader of a group of steelworkers from Katowice.

On September 17, representatives of the Independent Self-Governing Trade Unions (ISTU) (*Niezalezne Samorzadne Zwiazki Zawodowe* [NSZZ]) met in Gdansk and issued the following statement:

On September 17, 1980, at the headquarters of the Inter-factory Founding Committee of the Independent Self-Managed Trade Unions (NSZZ) in Gdansk, delegates from other areas of Poland assembled. At this meeting a review of the state of the NSZZ in various towns and regions of the country was carried out. Participants in the discussion were representatives from the Founding Committees of the NSZZ in Szczecin, Krakow, Katowice Steel Works, Mazowsze, Bydgoszcz, Walbrzych, Krosno, Elblag, Lodz, Prudnik, Jastrzebie Zdroj, Stalowa Wola, Wroclaw, Andrychow, Lublin, Bytom, Opole, Siemianowice, Torun, Tychy, Plock, Kolobrzeg, Poznan, Slupsk, Gorzow Wielkopolski, Rzeszow, Zywiec, Kozle, and Gdansk and also a representative of the NSZZ of Scientific, Technical, and Educational Workers in Krakow.

The review of organizational matters revealed that at the present over three million people from about three and a half thousand factories had joined or expressed the wish to join the NSZZ. The situation varies considerably and is dependent on the strength of workers' solidarity, the attitude of local authorities, and the sizes of the work places. While noting the progress being made in the foundation and organizational work of the independent autonomous unions, it was revealed that it is taking place in difficult conditions and must wrestle constantly with obstacles. In work places where a majority are female, the activities of the NSZZ are hampered by a policy of discrimination and by the pressure of the economic administration. In weaker or less numerous centers the emergence of the new unions is accompanied by fear of victimization and reprisals. Several actions of the authorities, such as detention and interrogation by the security forces of workers' delegates, or burdening them with police surveillance, create a source of new tensions. In most regions access to the mass media for the independent trade unions remains closed, and in certain areas there is evidence of disinformation techniques. The old unions from the CRZZ (Central Trade Union Council) try to conduct propaganda full of lies about alleged losses suffered by workers crossing over to join our unions. Local and regional authorities in many parts of the country do not carry into effect the spirit of the August agreements. Our unions grapple with local difficulties, while the management of many companies creates continuous obstacles to the activities of the NSZZ.

Independent Self-Managed Trade Unions have been formed throughout the whole country, also in many cities and regions which were not represented at the conference. Representatives of the NSZZ at the Gdansk Conference stated that establishment of new trade unions expresses the aims of the broad mass of working people of the whole country to possess independent and authentic representation. Concern was expressed that achieving conditions of the Agreement (concerning creation of new unions and guaranteeing no discrimination against them) was being met, at this inception stage, by many basic difficulties. Note was taken, at this meeting, of the resolution of the Council of State on September 13 which outlined the temporary principles of registration. Representatives of the NSZZ, while expressing uneasiness with certain sections of the resolution, stressed with considerable vigor that an efficient and speedy carrying out of that registration by the appointed channels was in the public interest.

The position of the NSZZ *vis-a-vis* the present state of the union, and concerning registration, was outlined in special declarations. The conference recognized that further activities of the NSZZ in the spirit of solidarity and caution require broad understanding and coordination. With this aim in mind, a Provisional Liaison Commission of NSZZ was set up. The proposal of the Gdansk NSZZ that the seat of the Commission be in Gdansk was accepted. During the first meeting of the Commission, Lech Walesa was elected Chairman. It will be the task of the Commission to organize common action for the NSZZ at the national level, and to insure the participation of the NSZZ in work on new legislation on trade unions, labor law, social and economic policies, and consultation and coordination in controlling the fruition of the agreements between workers and the government, as well as to conduct interventions. It will also be one of the tasks of the Liaison Commission to outline the methods of actions in the context of a homogeneous single union. The Liaison Commission will carry out the formalities of registering that union, which will encompass the Inter-Factory Founding Committees, and whose region of operation is the entire country (MacDonald, pp. 128-130).

The issue was whether to submit a single joint application for ISTU, and have a standardized charter for all the ISTUs, or risk registration refusal to separate unions, as happened to the Katowice Steelworkers. Walesa preferred a loose confederation and local autonomy [". . . We do not wish to make errors; therefore, we count on strong and independent regional organizations. They will be masters over everything which takes place in their territories. The Coordinating Committee must only coordinate and help, but not dictate solutions to the regional unions. We consider that the Commission's recommendations have to go down to the locals; there the final decisions will be made and forwarded back up "the line" (Offredo, p. 118). Walesa's statements in Polish are not always precise; therefore, my translations are not always literal; I try, however, to keep to the original as close as possible, without any effort to improve the style]. The representatives of the thirty-five unions affiliated with Solidarity formed a National Coordinating Commission (NCC) (Krajowa Komisja Porozumiewawcza).

The immediate tasks of the NCC were to organize the joint Solidarity for the whole of Poland, and to make sure that the new unions would have their say in forming the new trade union law, as well as influencing social policy, and controlling the implementation of Gdansk Accord.

Relations between Solidarity and the Government remained unsatisfactory. Solidarity complained about the obstructions of local authorities, the refusal to allow some men to form unions, the lack of media coverage or selective coverage, and false accusations about anti-socialist forces infiltrating the union's ranks. Similar accusations also appeared in the Soviet and East European press. Significantly, *Pravda* accused "subversive foreign forces," especially the AFL/CIO and some German organizations, of interfering in Polish internal affairs (*Pravda* [Moscow], September 20, 1980).

The next day, for the first time in the history of the Polish People's Republic (PPR) (*Polska Rzeczpospolita Ludowa* [PRL]), the national radio broadcast a Mass. And on the same day, the Polish bishops in a pastoral letter accused the information media of promoting false moral principles (Marxism), and appealed to parents to control their children's television viewing. Also on that date, the Chief Public Prosecutor, Lucjan Czubinski, announced that the investigation of some ex-dignitaries revealed mass bribery, mismanagment, and general corruption. The most eminent cases were those of Szczepanski, the ex-television boss; Stanislaw Radosz, the ex-Voievoda of Leszno; and Kazimierz Tyranski, the export-import manager of Minex. It was logical to expect that the continuing investigation would soon reach other Gierek proteges, and their ex-party boss himself.

Towards the end of September, the delegates of thirty-six unions agreed on statutes which were to be submitted to the Warsaw Voievodship court for registration. The statutes omitted mention of the leading role of PUWP.

The statutes were delivered by Lech Walesa to the Warsaw Voievodship for acceptance. However, registration was delayed, causing fear that Solidarity might be banned; the situation in the country became more tense. Solidarity's National Coordinating Committee announced that there would be a one-hour warning strike on October 3. The reasons for that decision, as formulated by the leading Warsaw region union (which was dominated by intellectuals), and by the Executive of the Integrated Founding Committee of the ISTU in Gdansk, were included in the statements they released:

On September 29, 1980 the Integrated Founding Committee of the Independent Self-Managed Trade Unions Solidarity in Gdansk decided to call a nationwide warning and solidarity strike for October 3. The strike is to start at 12 noon and last until 1 p.m. It has been called on the basis of Article 33, statute I, point 1 of the Union's Statute.

The strike has been called for the following reasons: the authorities are not fully implementing agreements concerning the following points: 1) wage agreements; 2) access by the independent, self-managed trade unions to mass media; and 3) non-obstruction of the activities of the independent, self-managed trade unions.

The executive of the unions of Mazowsze region decided that the following enterprises are to join the strike: Ursus (mechanical works), FSO (auto factory), TEWA (communications equipment), Nowotko, Polcolor (TV sets), MZK (city transport), MPT (taxis). In the above-named enterprises, local union Founding Committees will decide which depts. are to strike so as to minimize damage caused by the stoppages. The striking enterprises will hoist Polish national flags. The strike will start and end with the sounding of sirens. Only the predetermined depts. will take part. This will prove our strength, our discipline, and our organizing abilities. Those enterprises which do not take part in the strike, but which wish to demonstrate their solidarity with us, are requested to: 1) sound their sirens at noon and at 1 p.m.; 2) hoist Polish national flags; and 3) demonstrate their solidarity in other ways, as for example with posters or the wearing of armbands.

Independent Self-Managed Trade Unions
of the Mazowsze Region
Warsaw, September 30, 1980

On October 1, 1980 a meeting was held in the Gdansk Regional Governor's Office between the Deputy Prime Minister Jagielski and representatives of Party and Government, and representatives of Solidarity with its chairman, Lech Walesa. During the meeting, which lasted several hours, problems raised by Solidarity were discussed. The solution of these problems would allow the calling-off of the one-hour long warning strike which is to take place October 3. Representatives of Solidarity attended the meeting hoping that the authorities would suggest specific ideas which would remove the current difficulties concerning the organization and activities of the Independent Self-Managed Trade Unions, access to mass media, and consideration of workers' suggestions concerning the division of sums allocated for wage increases. Solidarity has suggested that agreements concerning wages be implemented no later than October 20. At first, agreement on these points seemed possible. A working group consisting of the representatives of both sides was set up to consider a joint communique. After an interval the government's side presented its own draft, which did not contain any specific proposals. Solidarity representatives stated that in the proposed text the representatives of the government had avoided any binding undertakings on the issues, which led to the strike being called.

On receiving the report of its representatives, the executive branch of Solidarity took the view that its representatives had done their best to convince the government of the necessity to remove the reasons for the strike. The executive states once again that it approached the negotiations with the honest intention of reaching agreement. The failure of the negotiations is therefore not its fault. The executive repeats Lech Walesa's statement, that: "Our union approaches the difficult political situation in the country with a proper seriousness, and, as we have stated on numerous occasions, wishes to contribute to a solution of the current crisis. This is, however, conditional on the full implementation of the agreements." Consequently, the strike we have called for does not constitute a departure from the agreements. It is an expression of protest against the creation of conditions which prevent the agreement from being put into practice.

Executive of the Integrated Founding Committee of the
Independent Self-Managed Trade Unions in Gdansk, Solidarity
Gdansk, October 1, 1980 (MacDonald, pp. 136-137).

The warning strike took place at the announced time and was a total triumph for Solidarity. At noon selected work places halted their activities for one hour. The other factory workers expressed sympathy by sounding factory sirens and displaying the national colors and emblems. Solidarity by now claimed membership of over six million Poles.

The Sixth Plenum of the Party took place the next day, after Solidarity's show of strength. Kania proposed some reforms. As errors of the past he cited over-investment, foreign debt, bad planning, and neglect of agricultural production. He stated that the Party leaders and Government ministers had too much power. The workers' strikes were not against socialism, but a protest against the previous Government's arrogant style and manner, and its habit of trumpeting false successes. Removed from its doubletalk, Kania's speech meant that the Party, an almost spiritual entity, still considered itself infallible, but its "earthly" representative Gierek had messed up the job and lied too much about it.

In the continuation of the plenary session, Gierek's old guard was decimated, and it was implied that he himself would soon be held accountable for his misdeeds.

In reference to the Solidarity warning strike, Kania explained that the authorities had agreed to give the strikers access to radio and television so they might explain their side of the story; but the union leaders went ahead with the walkout anyway.

The next day, delegates from thirty-nine regional Solidarity committees, in an open letter, objected to Kania's explanations and demanded thirty minutes of television time for rebuttal. In another letter addressed to Prime Minister Pinkowski, the delegates voiced their concern that Solidarity was still being denied legal status. Also, a resolution requesting fair coverage of ISTU activities by the government media was sent to Jagielski.

Throughout the following days the situation was tense. Walesa made a triumphant tour of Poland, as if to accent the recently displayed Solidarity muscle. In Krakow he was greeted as a new incarnation of Tadeusz Kosciuszko, the leader of the 1794 anti-Russian insurrection and participant in the American War of Independence.

There was some further shuffling of Government posts and some dismissals from the CC. But the all-important event was the verdict of the Warsaw court on the Solidarity registration, delivered October 24.

The Judge, Zdzislaw Koscielniak, no doubt acting on the Party's instructions, registered Solidarity as an independent, self-governing trade union, but deleted the statute sections dealing with the right to strike, and added the following paragraph:

> The union does not propose to play the role of the political party; it acknowledges the principle of communal ownership of the means of production, which is the foundation on which rests the existing social order in Poland; it acknowledges that the PUWP plays the leading role in the state; it does not undermine the established system of international alliances; it endeavors to guarantee the working people proper levers of control, freedom of expression, and defense of their interests (Radio Free Europe, *RAD Background Report/91* [Munich: Radio Free Europe, 1981], App. II, p. iv).

From a legal point of view, this was a curious statement, as it prescribed what the union was and particularly was not allowed to do instead of vice versa, leaving the rest to the constitution and law. Such a list might be prolonged *ad absurdum*. On the other hand, when the judge's paragraph was eventually deleted, it implicitly allowed the union to do those things that originally were so expressly forbidden.

The only rational explanation which occurs to me is that the paragraph in question was meant as a signal to Moscow not to worry, as the Soviet Union, directly and through its satellites, was conducting a campaign of intimidation in their press. According to numerous Soviet articles, all independent unions were against Leninist principles. The anti-socialist elements in Poland and their imperialistic masters were firmly condemned, and the theory of Brezhnev's doctrine fully affirmed.

The Czechoslovaks, with the background of their peculiar experience, were especially eloquent.

Solidarity rejected the court's verdict, making a sham of the judicial independence, and threatened to strike if the Supreme Court retained the original version. At the same time, it demanded access to the media, better food supplies, implementation of pay increases, and the release from customs of printing presses received from abroad.

In view of this grave situation, Kania and Pinkowski flew to Moscow. They returned after only a few hours, probably receiving agreement to Solidarity's requests. Brezhnev announced publicly that the communists and working people of the fraternal Polish nation were able to solve, on their own, the difficult problems of political and economic development.

The following days brought events almost boring in their repetitiveness. There were strikes everywhere. Solidarity accused the Government of sabotaging the Gdansk Accord, and of persecution of dissident workers. There were further changes in the Government, further dismissals from the CC. Kania acknowledged the positive role played by the Church in this crisis. (It seems that the Party and the Church suddenly found themselves strange bedfellows.) He promised that those guilty of past errors would be punished, and that those comrades who had failed them had already departed.

The Polish press printed a plethora of articles analyzing the "socio-economic" situation, blaming the past leaders of the Party and the present leaders of Solidarity for the generally-acknowledged mess in which Poland found herself.

The legal weekly, *Prawo i Zycie* (*Law and Life*), published some juicy details of life at the party's top. Maciej Szczepanski, it was gossiped, had golden knobs on his toilet, a private yacht, four mistresses (two of them Black), and an amazing collection of pornography, comparable to that of ex-King Farouk's (*Prawo i Zycie* [Warsaw], September 28, 1980). Gierek, it was whispered, had accumulated millions of dollars, deposited in Swiss banks, as had certain former dignitaries. *Pravda* criticized the Polish free trade unions as being bourgeois in character; and, strangely enough, a Polish Party paper, *Trybuna Ludu*, reported that, quite to the contrary, the reforms were a return to Leninist norms.

The Parliament met and showed some signs of revitalization. An interesting event for political observers of the Polish scene was the return of General Mieczyslaw Moczar to his power base at the Veterans' League (ZBoWiD). Moczar was a former Polish strong man and a competitor of Gierek.

The Minister of Justice, Jerzy Bafia, promised that a verdict in the case of the Solidarity registration would be given before November 10th.

The NCC of Solidarity and the Government representatives met at the palace of the Council of Ministers to discuss the controversial issues. However, the two sides failed to agree on a joint communique, in spite of the fact that Solidarity gained many concessions. For instance, the Government agreed to the publication of a weekly union newspaper; promised air time on television and radio; and released the impounded printing equipment. There was no promise, however, regarding the peasants' union, and no definite response on pay issues and market supplies.

The Government refused to sign Solidarity's version of the communique. Walesa stated that, if the Government kept all of its oral promises, this would be a great triumph for Solidarity—but there was nothing in writing. Evidently, Walesa and his followers were firm believers in written documents. The spirit of the British constitution was completely alien to the Polish workers, who did not wish to leave to the Government any freedom to maneuver.

Furthermore, Walesa threatened a series of strikes if the Supreme Court failed to register the union in accordance with the original charter. While the Government and Solidarity were wrestling, the economic situation of the country was getting progressively worse. Food rationing was introduced, but the long lines in front of shops soon became a permanent part of the Polish landscape. The Joint Polish-Soviet military maneuvers being held were conspicuously evident on Government television.

On October 10, the Supreme Court decided that the lower court had no right to eliminate any section of the Solidarity statutes, nor to make additions. However, in a dodge worthy of Judge John Marshall, it added two appendices to the statutes. One outlined the International Labour Organization conventions on collective bargaining; the other was the full text of the Gdansk Agreement, in which the leading role of the Party had been fully recognized. "We accomplished what we set out to accomplish on August 31 . . .," said Lech Walesa (Radio Free Europe, *Rad Background Report*, p. 113).

Indeed, the first phase of the Solidarity movement was successfully completed. Its significance, for the country and for the entire Eastern block, was tremendous. Free unions had been accepted by a governing communist party. The question remaining was whether or not the Party would or could adjust to the new *modus vivendi*.

Chapter 2

Triumph: More Freedom Than Bread

After Solidarity was registered, and the unprecedented (for the Eastern bloc) right to strike granted, there should have been a period of repose. The national interest demanded that Solidarity consolidate its gains and do something about the tragic economic situation of Poland, a country in whose affairs the union now had the formal right to participate. The Party, with "Big Brother" looking over its shoulder, needed time to lick its wounds, reorganize, and fight the economic decline. Common sense dictated that partnership was necessary in *odnowa*, the renewal.

This was not to be. A document from the Chief Prosecutor's office was leaked to Solidarity: Sapelo, the inside man, was arrested, together with the Solidarity printer, Narozniak. The Warsaw Solidarity branch demanded the immediate release of both men, and used the incident as a pretext for an attack on the internal security forces. Its demands went to the heart of the communist system: the political police were to have their budget reduced, a joint commission was to be set up to investigate abuses of power, and those guilty of repressions against the workers in 1970 and 1976 were to be tried. A strike alert was declared in Warsaw, and strikes actually erupted in numerous factories. The national leadership of Solidarity backed the Warsaw branch, but withdrew its support when the arrested were released.

Included in the Appendices are two interesting documents which supply useful background to these events. "On the Present Methods of Prosecution of Illegal Anti-Socialist Activity," which is signed by Czubinski, offers the official version; while that penned by Kuron, "Open Letter to Shipyard Workers and All Coastal Workers," gives the opposition's point of view.

Early in December, Kania, in an obvious allusion to Solidarity, stated in a meeting of the CC that there was no place for two centers of power in Poland; and, at the same time, purged additional members of the Politbureau, leaving only himself, Jaruzelski, Jagielski, and Jablonski from the original team. Previously, in a symbolic gesture, Jerzy Ozdowski, *Znak* Catholic Deputy, had been made a Vice-Premier. There were also several general purges in the Party; many others resigned, either as a protest against the present Party line or the Party itself, or simply to avoid being fired. There was also a kind of rebellion in the Party's rank-and-file; these members forged so-called horizontal structures contrary to the usual vertical structure of "democratic centralism" in Lenin's mode. A number of Party members actually joined Solidarity. Almost all of the working and social groups formed their own independent unions, students and *Pax* "progressive" Catholics included. On the other hand, Leszek Moczulski's League for Independent Poland dissolved itself.

The next conflict came over work-free Saturdays. The Government proposed to introduce them incrementally; Solidarity opposed; and, on January 17, 1981, only about 10 percent of the Polish workforce appeared at their stations. The Government completely capitulated, and agreed to free Saturdays and a forty-hour work week. Solidarity again was promised media coverage and limited participation in the governing process. There was no agreement on peasants' unions.

In February, Jozef Pinkowski, the Prime Minister, was dismissed and was replaced by General Wojciech Jaruzelski, the future successor to Kania. Jaruzelski, born in 1923, was deported with his family to the Soviet Union during World War II. There he joined the so-called I Polish Army, who fought the Germans along with the Red Army. Jaruzelski did not limit his fighting to the Germans, as he also battled the remainder of the Polish Resistance in 1945-1947. He joined the Party in 1948, worked in the political command of the Army, and became a member of the CC in 1964, joining the Politbureau in 1970. He is also Defense Minister.

After taking his post, Jaruzelski appealed to the nation for a three-month moratorium on strikes to restore normal economic functioning of the nation. He promised to continue the dialogue with Solidarity, and appointed Mieczyslaw Rakowski, the ex-protege of Gomulka and chief editor of *Polityka* (a Party weekly), as main negotiator.

The moratorium had Walesa's support, but it did not work too well. There was a strike in Zielona Gora to demand removal of allegedly corrupt local authorities, and another strike of similar nature in Bielsko Biala. About this time the Council of Ministers announced its project for partial payment of strike time, and there were threats of strikes which, however, did not materialize. The government team, under Jozef Kepa, flew to Bielsko Biala and signed an agreement to remove the officials of the local Voievodship, Jozef Labudek included.

More significantly, full payment for all strikers, now and in the future, was promised; and the promise was kept. It was easy to foretell that thousands of people would strike under any pretext to have government-paid vacations. The situation resembled in some ways that of unmarried mothers on American welfare rolls, who can count on receiving about $500 per month, more than an unskilled worker with a family.

The students gained a victory too. They were allowed free unions and organizations. The police were banned from campuses, the compulsory Russian language courses were abolished, and required courses in Marxism-Leninism reduced. On the administrative university boards, the students were granted one-third representation.

The peasants' Solidarities were mushrooming. Farmers in Rzeszow occupied the building of the Government Peasants' Party and rejected the Supreme Court offer of an associate status. They wanted a union of their own and threatened a strike of their own—refusal to deliver food (i.e., the definite starvation of the nation). The Court in its denial of registration was standing by the letter of the law. The Polish Work Code did not treat the individual peasants as workers, and, therefore, they could not be accepted as trade unionists. The peasants argued that, since most of their products went to the Government anyway, they were de facto state employees; further, workers on state and co-operative farms were allowed their unions.

Roughly 90 percent of land in Poland is in private hands. Farms are usually no larger than fifty hectares, and agricultural techniques are still backward. The horse still remains the main source of power. On the average, most peasants are elderly, since their children have largely emigrated to the towns. Indeed, they have little in common with city folk. From their point of view, it is obviously best to sell agriculture products as dear as possible, and to buy industrialized products, fertilizers included, as cheap as possible. For instance, they buy Government-subsidized bread to feed their cattle. The state is their main buyer, and in the past has kept food prices artificially low. In a sensible system, their bargaining position would be that of an interest group, not that of a union.

Early in March, all the rural Solidarities met at Poznan and amalgamated into one huge national organization, the Independent Self-Governing Trade Union Solidarity of the Individual Farmers.

This "peasant question" led to the events which overshadowed the IX Plenum of the CC, and the opening of a parliamentary session where Jaruzelski talked primarily about economic reform.

In the Bydgoszcz region, the peasants entered that town in military style, driving their tractors and occupying the headquarters of the Governmental Peasant Party (PZSL). This occupational strike was actively supported by the local "Solidarnosc," under a radical named Jan Rulewski. This young man had attended the Technical Military Institute (Wojskowa Akademia Techniczna). For refusing to vote for

Moczar and Korczynski, he was sent to a punishment company from whence he escaped abroad. He later returned to imprisonment, was released and re-enrolled at the university, but never finished his studies (*Tygodnik Solidarnosc* [Warsaw], October 9, 1981, p. 10). According to various articles in the Soviet press, Rulewski told his Russian military instructor that he had joined officer school to learn how to fight for Poland, and that the German occupation was better than the present Russian occupation. [This is an opinion expressed by quite a number of Polish people who are too young to remember the occupation.]

The peasants occupied the PZSL headquarters at about the same time a session of the Voievodship National Council (a regional administrative body to which six members of Solidarity were invited) was to take place. [The following version of events is based on an official report agreed upon by Solidarity NCC, and printed in *Trybuna Ludu* (Warsaw), March 30, 1981. The NCC affixed its addendum, of which the most important statement was that Walesa tried to reach, at crisis time, the Voievodship Building, but was refused telephone connection with Solidarity members.]

However, about twenty members of Solidarity appeared at the session, during which budget matters were supposed to be discussed, as well as candidatures for a new Voievoda. Solidarity was to take part in "free resolutions" towards the end of the meeting and then discuss agricultural problems.

The Chairman of the Voievodship Council, E. Berger, who was evidently afraid of potential conflict and the possibility of crowds arriving outside the building, stopped the session early in the afternoon, announcing that the date of the continued session would be given later. About forty council and Solidarity members remained outside the conference hall. The Vice-Voievoda, R. Bak, and the local prosecutor asked the Solidarity people to leave. When they refused, the militia was called in. The militiamen were unarmed. The Solidarity men linked their hands and made a circle, putting the women inside, and started to sing the national anthem. The protesters were bodily removed to the inner yard where three of them were brutally beaten. [The names of the victims were: Jan Rulewski, 37; Michal Bartoszcze, 68; and Marian Labendowicz, 25. All of them suffered brain shock and facial damage. Bartoszcze was taken to the hospital in serious condition.]

The Solidarity NCC rushed to Bydgoszcz, and there was a powerful and emotional wave of protest throughout the entire country, which included the newly-discovered toy of power strikes, a panacea for all problems. The Polish people were in a militant mood, in spite of the fact that "Sojuz 81," the annual Warsaw Pact maneuvers, were taking place on Polish soil. It was thought that, since the main Party leaders were abroad and the Soviet and Polish troops ready, the Bydgoszcz incident was a carefully planned provocation. Walesa was reported as saying that the situation was more dangerous than in August 1980, that brother would be hanging brother, and that there would not be enough lantern posts.

The NCC was not sure what to do. After two days of deliberation, it was decided to press the Government for an investigation, to seek punishment for the culprits. In addition, Solidarity wanted guarantees of freedom from alleged persecution, and the recognition of its rural sister. The previous demands were again enumerated (i.e., freedom for political prisoners, access to the official media, and the annulment of the Government decree which set a 50 percent limit on strike pay). If these demands were not granted, there would be a four-hour warning strike throughout Poland, followed by a general strike the following week.

On March 27, 1981 the four-hour warning strike took place. It was in fact a semi-general strike, and the atmosphere was orderly and calm. National flags were prominently displayed, and the national anthem and religious songs were sung.

A general strike was the ultimate weapon, an invitation to revolution, as was well realized by both the Party and Solidarity. During the IX Extraordinary CC Plenum, Mieczyslaw Rakowski, the chief negotiator and Deputy Prime Minister, said:

> We are threatened with a general strike. Its consequences must be cata-strophic, and they must destroy the line of agreement. We must realize that the general strike is crossing the precipice of a cliff. Nobody should delude himself otherwise. The general strike will mean that decisions about Poland will move from Party centers and maybe from NCC head-quarters, into the power of elementary forces (*Sztandar Modych* [Warsaw], March 30, 1981).

A general strike meant revolution and Russian intervention. Everybody would lose. Walesa stated:

> ...We have to be careful not to get involved in any adventure. If we shall strike—although I do not think there will be a general strike—then we should do so only inside factories, and never go out into the streets. If indeed there is a fraternal struggle, only a third party would be able to separate us. To maintain unity and calm we must win (*Zycie Warszawy*, March 29, 1981, p. 1).

Neither Rakowski nor Walesa could speak openly as Pole to Pole, but the whole charade meant that the Russians might intervene, and that they would be met with resistance. Strike headquarters were es-tablished in the Lenin Shipyard in Gdansk, and the local commands moved to the designated factories. Any police action would create thousands of fortresses in the country.

Under these tense circumstances, negotiations between the Govern-ment Commission under Rakowski and the Solidarity leadership under Walesa (accompanied by various experts, among them the celebrated opposition lawyer Wladyslaw Sila Nowicki) continued in Warsaw. Eventually, Solidarity agreed to accept the Government promise of punishing the Bydgoszcz culprits, after due process of law, and Walesa appeared on national television to call the strike off. The announcement was greeted with relief by many—but not by everyone.

Walesa was accused of monarchical autocracy by a prominent dissident, Karol Modzelewski, a member of the NCC who had resigned in protest; Jan Rulewski and Mariusz Labendowicz said Walesa wanted compromise at any price. Walesa's deputy, Andrzej Gwiazda, also criticized his boss and resigned. His resignation, however, was not accepted.

Walesa was further accused of tricking the NCC by moving to Gdansk the most militant members of its negotiating team, under the pretext that they would have to provide leadership in case he was arrested; and of having no authorization to lift the strike without endorsement of the entire NCC. Anna Walentynowicz also criticized Walesa.

However, Lech Walesa had shown much common sense, pointing to the political necessity of moving step by step: "We were doing a balancing act, and society was expecting compromise" (*Solidarnosc* [Gdansk], April 6, 1981, p. 10).

The NCC reluctantly agreed to the settlement, but said it would treat it only as a temporary document, a basis for further discussion. Meanwhile, the Bydgoszcz Voievoda resigned, and an official investigation of the incident was begun. In April the first issue of Solidarity's own weekly newsletter appeared under the editorship of Tadeusz Mazowiecki, one of the "experts"—and a man perhaps influential during Gdansk events of 1980. Further, a nationally televised meeting between the Government and Solidarity took place, where the union requested free access to the media, release of political prisoners, and registration of the rural Solidarity. On the latter point Government finally conceded, and the peasants' union was registered in May.

While events in Poland were gathering momentum, Russia was holding the XXVI Congress of the Soviet Communist Party. Leonid Brezhnev was duly re-elected, and noted that his Polish comrades were engaged in redressing a critical situation. The Soviet Union and its allies would not abandon "fraternal Poland" in its hour of need. Kania assured Leonid and others that the Poles would solve their problems on their own.

The situation in Poland was extremely painful. Food shortages grew steadily worse, as did the lines in front of shops. Rationing of a broad range of products was introduced, even for cigarettes and vodka. Rationing failed to ease the situation. There were complaints about mismanagement of food distribution: with more coupons circulating than goods to buy; and public gripes about a thriving black market and corrupt sales personnel. In post offices, stores, and ports thousands of food parcels sent to the Poles by their relatives abroad rotted away, or were pilfered by members of the distribution channels.

Productivity continued to decline. According to data from the government's main statistical office, in the entire period from January to July, 1981, the value of products sold through official outlets dropped 13.6 percent from the previous half year. Production of coal, the staple of Polish exports, decreased 21.3 percent; investment was down 21.1 percent; housing dropped 29.2 percent below the comparable periods; exports slid 18.3 percent; imports declined 9.4 percent; and so on.

The country was on the threshold of anarchy. Cardinal Wyszynski died, and the new Polish Primate, gnome-looking Archbishop Jozef Glemp, had neither Wyszynski's rank, prestige, authority, charisma, nor his experience. Walesa's appeals to stop the wildcat strikes were ignored. The numerous illegal newspapers which had appeared dared even to print Brezhnev's caricature and to criticize the Soviet Union. The jokes apparently enraged the good comrades at the Kremlin even more than the criticism; Soviet bureaucrats are noted for their humorlessness. *Krokodil*, the major Soviet magazine, publishes only caricatures of fat, cigar-smoking capitalists/imperialists, and those of the politicians from opposing blocks. The wave of Polish *odnowa* was followed by the usual denunciations in the Soviet press.

But long pent-up anti-Soviet feelings were beginning to surface. A few Soviet soldiers were beaten; red paint was dabbed on monuments to the Red Army; numerous songs and poems referring to the 19th-century tsarist occupation of Poland appeared, while Russian songs and films were boycotted by the Polish people.

Demonstrations for freeing political prisoners, as well as hunger marches and strikes, were erupting throughout the country. At the same time, crime began to rise, and in many cases the militia was afraid to intervene since actual criminals were being acclaimed as political prisoners and being rescued by mobs. There were even prison riots. Some streets were renamed after recent non-communist heroes such as Wladyslaw Sikorski, Aleksander Kaminski, and Eugeniusz Kwiatkowski. The Polish Academy of Sciences organized a scholarly session on the role in Polish history of Jozef Pilsudski, a pre-communist Polish leader. Monuments were erected to victims of the 1956 and 1970 tragedies, and to the Pope. It is curious to observe that in Polish official jargon such events are always referred to in an impersonal manner as "tragedies," as if they had been caused by some impersonal fate. Officials of the government attended some ceremonies honoring non-communist anniversaries, such as the regaining of Poland's independence, and of the Third of May Constitution. Books and leaflets expressing all shades of political opinion were printed legally or illegally.

Now, however, the Party was preparing for its Extraordinary Congress in July, as was promised during the IX Plenum. In the communist system, congresses are supposed to cure all ills. But this one was already "extraordinary," in that the delegates were being elected in more or less a democratic manner, and there was talk about statutory changes in the PUWP. The similarities to Dubcek's Czechoslovakia were obvious to everyone; the Kremlin comrades no doubt were mumbling Lenin's famous question: *"Shto delat?*—What to do?" Meanwhile, the Party sent a letter on the eve of the PUWP XI Plenum, signed by the CC of CPSU. The key paragraphs are as follows:

...An unusual and grave danger hangs over Poland, which is simultaneously a danger to the sovereign existence of that state. If the worst happens and power falls into the hands of the enemies of socialism, if Poland loses the security of the socialist community, the greedy hands of the imperialists would immediately reach for her. And who then would guarantee the independence of Poland, her sovereignty, and her frontiers? Nobody....

...Allowing successful attempts at defaming and paralyzing the security forces and militia is equal to disarmament of the socialist state, and delivering it into the hands of the class enemy. [*Zycie Warszawy*, June 11, 1981, p. 1. An outside reader would certainly think that the main enemies of Poland are American "imperialists" and their German "lackeys."]

The above is not a parody of Soviet jargon written by an anti-communist, but an authentic letter, dated June 5, and printed in the Polish press on June 11 (i.e., after the XI Plenum ended). Already, even before it was made public, the Soviet ideologue, Mikhail Lebedev, a doctorate candidate in Legal Science, referred to the letter in a radio show aired in Poland by Moscow. Lebedev told the Polish nation that:

Everything the Soviet people and state achieved in building socialism and communism is connected with the leading role of the Marxist-Leninist party; as is all its success in creating the economic might of the USSR and the consolidation of the enormous international prestige of the land of Soviets.

...Life affirms that each deviation from Leninist principles, each weakening of the party, leads to its ideological disarmament. *Rude Pravo* stresses this while analyzing the noted CPC document, "The Teaching of Crisis Development." This involves activization, revisionism, and right-wing opportunism. The field is opened for an offensive by reactionary forces inside the country and the class enemy from abroad. This, among other things, is what happened in Czechoslovakia (U.S. Foreign Broadcast Information Service, *Daily Report*, July 8, 1981, p. F4).

The allusions here are clear enough; let us also remember the quotation from Brezhnev at the end of the letter from the CC of CPSU saying that Socialist and fraternal Poland would not be left alone in her troubles; this meant that the Soviet Union would not allow its small brother to be hurt. This was an ominous sign.

The Soviets' concern was duly acknowledged by Stanislaw Kania:

The concerns and anxieties of the fraternal parties about the direction in which the Polish situation is developing, their fears of the consequences of a prolonged crisis, and their fears of the consequences it may have for the socialist countries, are fully justified. And for these reasons, we pay the greatest attention to the fears of our Soviet comrades and to their well-wishing remarks (*Zycie Warszawy*, June 10, 1981, p. 3).

General Wojciech Jaruzelski put the matter in global terms:

> ...Disarmament talks are at an impasse. The initiatives of the Soviet Union and the socialist countries are not sown on fertile ground. The temper and the scale of armaments imposed on us by the imperialistic military complex is growing. Conflicts or their possibilities are arising on various continents. In this situation, every unstable point creates a potential danger. Poland's place in Europe and our position in the Warsaw Pact are special; and therefore, what is happening in our country—the destabilization of Europe—threatens to upset the equilibrium on a much greater scale. On this continent of Europe, it is impossible to stay neutral. It is not by accident that the CC of CSUP puts such emphasis on the question of our state borders, and on Polish independence (*Zycie Warszawy*, June 11, 1981, p. 3).

While the XI Plenum was being held, there was also a session of Parliament. The government submitted a number of bills, the most important concerning the workers' councils, the structure of state enterprises, and the new price policy.

Talks about reforms, new styles of administration, revamping of the Party, and many other things described as *odnowa*, became a part of everyday life. But whenever the Party tried to introduce reforms, on paper or in reality, it was rebuked by Solidarity and the nation for not going far enough, as if the Party could somehow deliver an economic miracle or escape the overwhelming influence of the "fatherland of socialism" (i.e., the Soviet Union).

On July 15, the IX Extraordinary Conference of the United Workers Party started its deliberations. Although there were the usual lengthy and dull reports and speeches, the main issue was the election of the new leadership. The event was unusually suspenseful, since this was the first time in the history of the Eastern bloc that some uncertainty existed as to the outcome of the selection of the First Secretary. Soviet "friendly concern" expressed by the CC of CPSU indicated that Kania's candidature was favored. But the Soviet Union could not be really sure, either, since most of the delegates to the conference were new and somewhat democratically chosen. Also, the election for First Secretary was to be democratic itself, with a number of competing candidates. Prague spring might indeed be repeated in Polish summer.

However, the election brought no surprises. Stanislaw Kania was re-elected by a margin of 1,939 votes over his main opponent, Kazimierz Barcikowski, with 60 votes invalid. The two other candidates, Stefan Olszowski and Mieczyslaw Rakowski, refused to run.

The votes for members of the Politbureau were: Kazimierz Barcikowski, 186 votes; Tadeusz Czechowicz, 170; Jozef Czyrek, 187; Zofia Grzyb, 177; Wojciech Jaruzelski, 189; Hieronim Kubiak, 150; Jan

Labecki, 162; Mieczyslaw Maksymowicz, 42; Zbigniew Messner, 176; Miroslaw Milewski, 167; Kazimierz Miniur, 57; Jozef Mitak, 45; Stefan Olszowski, 186; Stefan Paterek, 35; Tadeusz Porebski, 170; Albin Siwak, 133. Thus, Jaruzelski was the most popular, while Maksymowicz, Miniur, Mitak, and Paterek lost [*Trybuna Ludu* (Warsaw), July 20, 1981, p. 2 . The Politbureau members were mostly men in their fifties, "apparatchiks," with Party university education. Zofia Grzyb had the double distinction of being the only woman and the only Solidarity member in the Politbureau. Hieronim Kubiak is an expert on Polish emigration, and has visited the United States on various scholarships.]

Five former members of the Politbureau were not elected to the new Central Committee of the Party: Henryk Jablonski (Chairman of the State Council), Mieczyslaw Jagielski (Deputy Premier), Mieczyslaw Moczar (Chairman of the Supreme Chamber of Control, and Veterans' boss), Tadeusz Grabski (Chairman of the Commission established to find those guilty of mismanaging the country), and Tadeusz Zabinski (First Secretary of the Katowice Region). Also, some alternate members of the CC, former CC secretaries, and the Warsaw and Krakow First Secretaries, lost their sinecures.

The chief victim, however, was Gierek and his group: Edward Gierek, Edward Babiuch, Jerzy Lukasiewicz, Zdzislaw Grudzien, Jan Szydlak, Tadeusz Pyka, and Zdzislaw Zandarowski, were all expelled from the Party.

It is difficult not to feel some amount of sympathy for Gierek, the man who gave Poland some measure of prosperity, and a man who refused to use force against his countrymen, or call for Soviet help. In spite of his mismanagement and errors, he was not responsible for the world economic crisis of which Poland was only a part. Expulsion from the Party is the equivalent of civil death; it is much better never to have belonged to the Party, even to be an open anti-communist, than to be removed from its ranks, particularly from a position of authority.

The age of the new Politbureau averaged fifty years, in contrast to the average of thirty to forty years in the Solidarity leadership, indicating that the Solidarity-Party conflict was also, in part, a generation struggle.

The IX Extraordinary Congress issued the following appeal to the nation which, at the same time, was its program of action:

> Fellow countrymen. The homeland is in need. A profound economic, social, and political crisis is tormenting our country. There is danger to the secure existence of the nation and to the future of the state. Let us join forces to avert the danger which hangs over Poland. Today's crisis is not a result of the socialist system. On the contrary, it is the departure from the ideological precepts of socialism, from the ideas which have always guided the workers' movement, that has brought disaster to Poland. Those responsible for this are men who, while standing at the helm of the Party and of the state, betrayed ideas they voiced. The party is getting rid of them. It

is determined to continue to the end the process of bringing to account those responsible. Today, however, the most urgent issue for the nation is to find a way out of the crisis. We must look ahead. We must not allow the considerations of past evils to paralyze the will and ability of our country (U.S. Foreign Broadcast, p. 30).

The Party had promised to achieve economic equilibrium, to reform the economy, to develop agriculture, to fight for democracy in the state and for the needs of the new generation, as well as women's rights. But,

Only a Marxist-Leninist party is capable of guaranteeing the success of socialist renewal and implementation of the line of social agreement, of ensuring the lasting security of the state and the sovereign existence of the nation (Ibid., p. 31).

The Party partially reformed itself, accepting corrections of its statutes which, according to the official declaration, strengthened the role of basic party links, and introduced greater rights for the party's elective organs as opposed to executive bodies. The elective bodies were now under some voters' control.

On the whole, however, the Party's declarations, speeches, and reports were greeted with the usual cynical disbelief. The credibility gap was too deep. Perhaps more convincing was Jaruzelski's statement:

In the present difficult period our Armed Forces have not been shaken. They have maintained their cohesion and discipline. They are always ready to defend the fatherland and its socialist achievements (*Trybuna Ludu* [Warsaw], July 20, 1981, p. 5).

Before progressing further, perhaps, we should say a few words about Grabski's Commission; Grabski, as was noted, lost his position for not being severe enough on his ex-comrades. The Commission was established by the X Plenum in April 1981, and its task was to determine the level of responsibility of the members of former leadership for the Polish crisis. The chronological period under investigation was from 1970 to 1980.

The Commission concluded in its report to the Extraordinary Congress that there was, indeed, a Gierek cult; that his proteges, especially Franciszek Szlachcic and Edward Babiuch, had too much influence over the man; that decisions were made in a dictatorial manner; and that the role of the Politbureau was limited, and those who opposed Gierek and his clique were discriminated against and cajoled. There was no worthwhile planning or analysis of the situation. The real economic situation was falsified by propaganda emphasizing successes, the true data being hidden from the Party and the people.

The Commission investigated a number of ex-dignitaries who abjectly confessed their guilt in a tone reminiscent of the Moscow Trials. Two of them, Jerzy Olszewski, the ex-Minister of Foreign Trade, and Edward

Barszcz, of the Building Ministry, committed suicide under suspicious circumstances. Numerous criminal and Party sanctions were applied to these men; they were also stripped of their many medals, decorations, and even diplomas. Gierek and his colleagues now faced legal proceedings. Gierek had a house in Katowice, built with state funds, and another such home in Ustronie Slaskie.

The first year of the crisis was drawing to a close, with no improvement in the situation. In addition to shortages of food, there were now shortages of soap, detergents, toilet paper, even newspapers (except for the Party organ, *Trybuna Ludu*). To buy furniture or appliances, people had to prepay the amount and then wait for about three years for promised delivery. Thousands started to leave the country, legally or illegally, much to the inconvenience of nearby Austria, and to the discomfort of the overcrowded West.

The Government decided to cut meat rations from about eight pounds to 6.5 pounds per capita per month. The first "hunger march" took place in Kutno. Next, almost the entire population of the large industrial city of Lodz came out into the streets for four days. Their signs read: "We do not want to be hungry. We want work"; "How do you eat your coupon, with fork or spoon?" The protests culminated in a procession of women and children. Similar marches took place in Szczecin and Warsaw.

In Warsaw, thousands of demonstrators blocked traffic, and the militia was afraid to intervene, as the workers organized a guard of their own. There was a strike in which about half a million employees participated. A million workers went on strike in the mine districts of Silesia (*Tygodnik Solidarnosc* [Warsaw], August 21, 1981, p. 1). In almost all the cities and towns people demonstrated against the Government's inability to stop the economic decline. Many of them thought that the Government in conjunction with the Russians wanted to starve the nation into submission.

"Solidarnosc" did appeal for an end to the work stoppages, and even for an end to work-free Saturdays:

> NCC asks all the members of the union, all the workers of the country to sacrifice our own free time to save ourselves; let us work the eight free Saturdays till the end of this year. We know that this is unprecedented in free union countries.
>
> We appeal to all the organizations and union authorities not to undertake isolated protesting activities (Ibid.).

The union, however, was not able or willing to stop grass roots movements. Thus, in order to secure its commanding position, or, if one prefers, to keep the demonstrations peaceful and orderly, it was forced in every case to join them.

A year had passed since the Gdansk accord; the Government published the following communique, which contains, in the author's opinion, a relatively fair assessment of the developments:

In accordance with the agreements, decisions were adopted as a result of which the wage fund rose by about 260 billion zlotys. From this sum, increases were made in the wages of all working people and also in old-age and disability pensions. Other social security payments were also increased, and the work week was cut. In total, up to 1985, the government will have to spend more than 1.4 trillion zlotys in accordance with the concluded agreements. Part of this sum, about 800 billions, will be spread out over the entire five-year-plan period, particularly in the fields of housing construction and social security. But the money for raising wages, social security benefits, and the incomes of self-employed peasants [*krestyaneyedinolichniki*], totalling about 607 billion, will have to be spent in the near future.

This is quite a considerable expense. It will require the elimination of the crisis in the economy. Possibilities for improving the people's living conditions depend on economic growth and particularly on the results of everyone's labor.

The social agreements were of the nature of bilateral obligations. They were supposed to result in increased efficiency of production and the raising of labor productivity.

Unfortunately, this has turned out differently. Social tensions and the worsening of the crisis in the national economy are calling into question faith in Poland as a partner in economic cooperation, limiting the government's freedom of economic action. The Polish authorities also took a number of steps to fulfill agreements in the social field. The broad democratization of public life and the consistent process of social renewal are going far beyond the scope of the agreements. They have become an achievement of the PZPR, confirmed at the ninth congress as a lasting gain of Poland's working people.

The activities of the independent and self-governing trade unions are developing freely. The government has not really had their active support in economic actions. Throughout the past year, there has been persistent tension as a result of various pressures and demands, protests and actions by branches of Solidarity. This has had an extremely negative effect on the country's socioeconomic stabilization, and on the possibility of implementing the agreements in any significant way. Contrary to the Gdansk, Szczecin, and Jastrzebie agreements and to the trade union charter, the Solidarity bulletins, leaflets and posters call into question our alliances, the leading role of the party, and the structural principles of the Polish People's Republic. The actions of certain Solidarity branches amount to deliberate attacks on state institutions and the administrative and economic authorities, limiting their scope of activity. That is, they are directed at weakening and paralyzing authority. This cannot fail to affect its efficient functioning and its efforts to overcome the crisis and improve the people's living conditions.

The fulfillment of the social agreements will be possible only upon the bilateral implementation of the social contract, directing all forces to the solution of the most important economic problems, and the constructive cooperation of all the country's social forces.

The trade union committee document contains assessments of the implementation of the points in the Gdansk, Szczecin, and Jastrzebie agreements of significance for the whole country; and an assessment of the financial consequences ensuing from the implementation of the Industrial Branch Trade Unions.

Here are certain data contained in the document:

In the field of wage regulation, changes were made to collective agreements and the problem of working hours; wages were raised for all workers as of November 1, 1980, and at the same time the minimum wage was raised to 22,400 zlotys per month....

...The date for introducing the 40-hour work week is to be decided in talks between the government and the trade unions this year. For 1981, the introduction of a 42-hour work week was agreed....

...In the field of social security benefits: from January 1, 1981, old-age and disability pensions were raised by 500 zlotys—a number of other pensions were also increased. Within the framework of the reform of the family allowances system, more assistance is being given to families with relatively low incomes, particularly to those with several children.

In the field of health service: in 1981, 36 percent more money has been allocated to the needs of health and social security than in 1980. There are 177 planned projects connected with the health service, of which 32 are already in operation.

In the field of labor protection: the principle of payment of compensatory benefits has been introduced to workers suffering industrial injuries or contracting industrial diseases, for the entire period of employment at the enterprise in question. Pneumoconiosis has been recognized as an industrial disease....

...The current state of affairs regarding capital investment does not permit, as intended, providing apartments in the present five-year plan period for all those who should have received them by the end of 1980. Nor can the waiting-list period for an apartment be reduced to five years.

In the field of improvement to market supplies: measures have been taken to reduce the social effects of the worsening provision of goods to the population, primarily in the field of foodstuffs. However, in spite of the introduction of meat coupons, it has not been possible to raise deliveries to a level at which the coupons can be fully honored during their validity dates. To improve the position of the market, the government has formed an extraordinary commission to combat speculation.

In the field of the activities of the independent, self-governing trade unions: on September 13, 1980, the Council of State adopted a decision on the question of...trade unions.

On November 1, 1980, the Independent, Self-Governing Trade Union Solidarity was registered, and by August 15, 1981, 84 trade unions had been registered. The independent, self-governing Solidarity trade union for self-employed peasants was also registered.

A draft law on trade unions has been sent to the *Sejm* and is now being worked on by *Sejm* commissions.

Drafts of basic decisions on important problems of the working people are sent to the trade unions for review.

An opportunity has been created for the trade union press to function. The weekly *Solidarnosc* is produced with a circulation of 500,000 copies.

An opportunity has been provided for the Solidarity trade unions to have radio and television time.

The bill on trade unions...touches on methods of solving collective disputes, responsibility for breaches of the law, etc.

The government is fully observing the principles of the solution of disputes formulated in the bill on trade unions. Unfortunately, branches of the Solidarity trade union have repeatedly breached the principles laid down in its charter. A number of strikes have been called without preliminary negotiations.

In the field of decisions of a general nature, the *Sejm* has passed a law on controlling publications and public performances, which will come into effect on October 1, 1981.

A joint commission of representatives of the government and the episcopate, which is intended to help normalize relations between the state and the church in the interests of the country's development and the unity of its citizens, has begun its activities. Sunday Mass is broadcast every week.

Work on the printing law, which will determine the legal norms for the functioning of the press, radio, and television and also the principles of public control over them, is continuing.

The Ministry of Labor, Wages, and Social Matters has granted the right to return to work to persons dismissed for strike activities in the period 1970-1980.

A draft economic reform has been worked out, on the basis of which the Ninth PZPR Congress adopted the "Guidelines for Economic Reform." It has been passed on to the *Sejm* by the government. Bills on state enterprises and the self-management of collectives have also been sent to the *Sejm*. A report has been produced on the state of the national economy. The latter was adopted by the *Sejm* last July.

In conclusion, the document prepared by the Committee on Trade Unions Affairs notes that, in view of the worsening economic situation, the adopted measures must be thought about again. They must also be adapted to the new conditions ensuing from the economic reform.

The Gdansk, Szczecin, and Jastrzebie agreements contain bilateral obligations. The government is counting on the full implementation of the obligation undertaken by the independent trade union Solidarity as a result of the social agreements, and hopes that it will fully observe the principles contained in its charter that it voluntarily accepted.

The government is counting on the possibility of cooperation in partnership with all the trade unions in solving the difficult and urgent problems, and on their mutual cooperation in this field.

It is this will of cooperation in partnership, in the spirit of the policy of social renewal, that the government is reaffirming (U.S. Foreign Broadcast, pp. G46-G48).

Solidarity, of course, disagreed with the Government communique, blaming the Government for the conflict situation and for deliberately failing in its obligations. By now the union was planning a conference of its own in two parts; delegates would return to their regions to report and discuss the ideas and matters proposed at the first session, then resume deliberations after receiving input locally.

The delegates met in Gdansk on September 5, and before the

Congress opened, the new Primate of Poland, Archbishop Jozef Glemp, celebrated the Mass. [It was proposed that there would be daily morning Mass; however, that was too much and the delegates decided to dispense with such ceremony.] Before the deliberations started, 892 delegates representing a membership of about 9.5 million unionists sang the national anthem, "Poland is Not Dead Yet," and the religious song, "God Who Created Poland." In his opening speech, Lech Walesa said among other things:

> I am not a diplomat, so I shall state this openly. Until the last moment before this conference started, many actions were carried out and many words said which could be avoided. Replies to many important questions are expected from us. We shall here debate them. But we too expect an answer to the fundamental question. A year ago we said that we talked to each other as a Pole to a Pole. Now after these twelve months of conflicts, we want to know whether we shall continue to talk in this manner. Is the moment of understanding upon us, that it will be impossible to reverse that road which we opened in August, and that Solidarity will not allow itself to be divided or destroyed? (*Kultura* [Warsaw], September 20, 1981, p. 7).

The delegates debated in a jubilant mood, many of them in funny hats. Everything ran smoothly. There were teams of interpreters who translated the proceedings almost immediately. Foreign correspondents appeared *en masse*, as did Polish journalists. To spite the Government, Solidarity did not allow Polish television crews. A special Congress daily, *Glos Wolny*, ran an English edition. There was a press information desk working efficiently, and legal and illegal books and publications could be purchased. Security guards were placed at all entrances. Inside and outside the spacious "Olivia" sports hall hung huge banners spelling "Solidarnosc."

Andrzej Celinski, Secretary of the NCC, presented its report to the delegates. According to the report, the leadership of the union saw that Poland faced an economic catastrophe, due primarily to mismanagement and faulty policies dating well before the period of July-August 1981. The most urgent problems were food shortages, housing, transportation, and inflation. This first Congress of Solidarity was closing the initial phase of the union, which now represented 9.5 million members, and constituted the most powerful social movement in Poland. A revolution had taken place in Poland. The authorities were afraid of society and reforms. The protests of July and August were directed against injustice and lies, arbitrary decisions and orders by the authorities, and the constantly deteriorating economic situation which resulted from the activities of pre-August state authorities, and from the consequent lack of consistent government policy since August, 1980. The union was constantly being dragged into conflict situations, moving from one to the next, almost from the beginning. Not only the interests of working people and those of the union, but the very existence of Solidarity itself and the country's destiny, had been placed in a state of utmost danger.

Celinski later lauded the opposition groups and the Church for their role in the renewal of Poland, and referred to a campaign of slander against Solidarity, stating that the monopoly of information and expression on television and radio violated the rights of society. The speech ended with the note that the work of the union benefited Poland, and should meet with the Government's approval (Based on various reports in the U.S. Foreign Broadcast Information Service, *Daily Report*, September 8, 1981).

This report was bold and undiplomatic in its challenge, both to the PUWP and the Soviet Union implicitly; even more careless was the appeal of the delegates to the workers of Eastern Europe:

> Message to the working people of Eastern Europe. The delegates gathered in Gdansk at the first Conference of the Independent Self-Governing Trade Union Solidarity send greetings and words of support to workers of Albania, German Democratic Republic, Rumania, Hungary, and to all the nations of the Soviet Union.
>
> As the first independent trade union in our post-war history, we feel a strong sense of our communal fate. We assure you that in spite of the lies spread in your countries, we are the authentic 10-million member organization of working people which was created as a result of labor strikes. Our goal is to fight for improvement in the lives of all working people. We support those of you who have decided to take the path of difficult struggle for free trade unionism. We believe that shortly your and our representatives will be able to meet and exchange their union experiences (*Tygodnik Solidarnosc* [Warsaw], September 18, p. 6).

This Solidarity message, coupled with other resolutions, deeply embarrassed the CC of PUWP, and upset Kania's balancing act. The Politbureau immediately issued a statement charging that Solidarity had fallen under the influence of Western saboteurs, and had become a subversive political force. The message to the working people of Eastern Europe was described as a mad act of provocation against the allies of socialist Poland and an encouragement for an anti-Soviet campaign. Solidarity was denounced for breaking its agreement with the Government, and adopting a program of political opposition aimed at the vital interests of the state, a course which would lead to national tragedy, ending in bloodshed. (It must be mentioned here that allusions to the civil war had been constant for many months in the Government press.) But the Party would defend Poland, and the state would use all the necessary means at its disposal for that purpose.

The Solidarity message, of course, implied some sort of international labor organization in Eastern Europe. This vision was not quite to the taste of the Kremlin, who preferred to keep its slogan "proletarians of the world unite," only on the mastheads of its newspapers. The Soviets protested the document as being counter-revolutionary interference in their internal affairs, and TASS described the Solidarity Congress as an orgy of anti-socialist and anti-Soviet elements. Solidarity once again was accused of conspiring with foreign "imperialists" in an attempt to seize power in Poland and restore the bourgeoise system.

Mass meetings were "spontaneously" organized in Moscow and Leningrad, where workers condemned the Polish Solidarity. The satellite press also expressed its horror at the thought of free unions in their countries.

The Polish Government press joined the choir; and a statement from the Polish Foreign Ministry claimed that Solidarity had struck a blow against the Polish national interest, and had interfered in the internal affairs of other socialist states. The inspirers of the message had violated the principal foundations of Polish foreign policy, striking directly against the Polish *raison d'etat*.

The Soviet ambassador to Poland, Aristov, handed Kania and Jaruzelski a note almost immediately after the Solidarity message, a note which was made public only on September 18th. According to Radio Free Europe, the Politbureau seriously considered approaching Parliament to pronounce a state of war on the basis of Article 33 of the Polish Constitution; a rather difficult request, as that Article states clearly:

> ...A decision concerning the declaration of a state of war may be adopted only in the event of armed aggression having been committed against the Polish People's Republic... (*Constitution of the Polish People's Republic* [Warsaw: Krajowa Agencja Wydawnicza, 1981], p. 26).

or in pursuance of international agreements. But there was still peace in the country, in spite of the storm brewing in Russia.

On the other hand, the Council of State is empowered to proclaim martial law almost at will. Radio Free Europe reports, usually reliable [from loose mss. pages in the author's possession], claim that proclamation of the state of emergency was torpedoed by the suddenly independent parties of the so-called National Front.

Therefore, the Politbureau limited itself to issuing a communique which openly threatened bloodshed. Mieczyslaw Rakowski, the chief Government negotiator with Solidarity, stated that the line of dialogue between two political powers was lost. But the very next day Olszowski, in a televised speech, announced that all patriotic forces were invited to participate in the Front of National Unity; the offer included Solidarity.

Olszowski stated that Poland had been developed with Soviet help. Polish industry was intricately linked with the Soviet industrial complex, with Poland importing over $13 million in oil, iron and cotton from the USSR, not to mention food and monetary loans. The Soviet Union could manage very well without Polish supplies, but not vice versa.

What was not said openly, but well understood by most parties, was that the Soviets need not intervene militarily in Poland. It would be sufficient to cut off essential supplies. The same idea was implied in still another letter from the comrades of the CC CPSU. [An interesting point occurs. If the Solidarity message was an interference in Soviet internal affairs, how would we describe the numerous letters from the Kremlin, its "friendly" instructions on how to deal with Solidarity aired to Poland, visits of Soviet dignitaries on the eves of the PUWP Plenums and Conferences, and finally, the numerous maneuvers and troop movements along the border?] That letter made clear the message that the Kremlin had lost patience with the inability of Polish authorities to halt the danger to the system. It openly rebuked the Party and Government for their indecision and passivity. One such message, which was not made public in the Polish press, according to the *New York Times*, referred to the cutting off of Soviet supplies (*New York Times*, September 19, 1981). According to that letter, time and again the attention of PUWP had been drawn to the mounting wave of anti-Sovietism in Poland. The four occasions when the matter was referred to were specifically enumerated: meetings between the Polish and Soviet leadership in Moscow and in Warsaw in April; the earlier warning letter from the CC CPSU; and the Crimean meeting between Brezhnev and Kania in August.

The union was not to be browbeaten, however. In many factories resolutions were adopted condemning Soviet interference and inviting Soviet workers to come to Poland to see for themselves what was going on.

The other resolutions of the Solidarity conference were of lesser importance, mostly *ad hoc* subjects. One of these concerned the right to strike for television employees (they were specifically forbidden by Government to strike), universities and the education of youth, condemnation of the end to the Bydgoszcz accident investigation, passports and freedom to travel, etc. However, the other significant resolution (beside the "Message") was one calling for the Government to hold a popular referendum on workers' self-management, the main point of which was the right of workers to have managers to their liking. The other rather rhetorical resolution requested free elections to the local Voievodship Councils.

The conference ended its long and complicated deliberations by issuing the following declaration:

> The overwhelming purpose of ISTU Solidarity is creation of respectable conditions of life in economically and politically independent Poland. The question concerns life free from poverty, exploitation, terror, and lies, in a democratic society in which the law is respected. Today the nation is expecting:
> 1) Improvement of food supplies through control over its production, distribution, and prices, in collaboration with the Rural Solidarity.
> 2) Economic reform through creation of the authentic workers' council, and liquidation of party *nomenklatura* [*nomenklatura* refers to the party

principle by which only its members can obtain certain jobs], and introduction of effective economic mechanisms.

3) Truth through the control by society of mass media, and the removal of lies from Polish schools and culture.

4) Democracy through free elections to *Sejm* and National Councils.

5) Justice through ensuring equality in the law, and freeing those imprisoned for their opinions, and the defense of those who are persecuted for their union and publishing activities.

6) Redemption of the endangered national health through environmental protection, more development in health services, and rights for the handicapped.

7) Coal for the people and industry through guaranteeing miners proper conditions of work and life.

These aims we shall reach through the coherence of our Union and the solidarity of its members. The activities of various forces which create feelings of internal danger will not take from us the will to fight for the ideals of August '80, and the realization of the agreements of Gdansk, Szczecin, and Jastrzebie (*Tygodnik Solidarnosc* [Warsaw], September 18, 1981, p. 1).

This declaration was almost as significant as the American Declaration of Independence, since the realization of free elections would effectively finish communist rule in Poland immediately. Russian fears, and the subsequent ouster of Kania, should have come as a surprise to no one. Jaruzelski announced a state of military preparedness. The Council of State declared its eagerness to defend socialism, etc. But nothing happened. The delegates returned peacefully to their homes while the stream of abuses from Moscow and her satellites continued. The Party's Politbureau issued the following statement:

Poland's political situation is developing in a dangerous direction. The state of economy is steadily deteriorating and the living conditions of the people are becoming ever more difficult. The arresting of these processes is a national must. The 9th extraordinary congress of the PUWP formulated in its resolutions a program for leading Poland out of the crisis.

We are providing possibilities for constructive participation in the country's life of all the social forces based on socialism. Such possibilities have been also opened up for Solidarity, the new trade union. That is why its first congress aroused such interest and hope in numerous circles of society. These hopes have been dashed. The course and the resolutions of the first part of the congress elevated adventurist tendencies and phenomena which had occurred within Solidarity—although they seemed to be only extreme trends—to the rank of the official program of the entire organization.

Thus, the agreements concluded in Gdansk, Szczecin, and Jastrzebie have been unilaterally broken. They have been replaced by a program of political opposition which hits at the vital interests of the Polish nation and the state, and marks the direction towards confrontation with threats of bloodshed.

The congress has virtually disappropriated the working class from influence on and co-responsibility for their organization in favor of interests, plans, and aims represented by opposition, adventurist, and counter-revolutionary groupings, including the so-called Workers Defense Committees and the so-called Confederation of Independent Poland. This has come about through such persons who are in touch with and act under the influence of Western subversion centers aimed against socialist Poland, as well as extreme groups of the workers movement financially and technically aided by those centers.

This is the truth. It must be brought home to the entire working class, to all working people and all milieus, and, especially, to the members of Solidarity in whose name the course towards a new national tragedy has been plotted.

In spite of a tense situation, the Political Bureau of the PUWP Central Committee reaffirms its readiness and the necessity of building an alliance with all, and an understanding with anyone who is not against socialism and who has at heart the cause of the motherland and its rescue.

We shall defend socialism in the same way as we defended Poland's Independence. The state will use for this defense any means which will be called for by the situation.

The above sentence was one of many portents of the events of December 13th.

Before the Congress was to reconvene, Wojciech Jaruzelski announced in his address to Parliament that he had ordered the militia and special army detachments to crack down on the deepening anarchic tendencies, hooliganism, anti-sovietism, and anti-statism. The army and militia patrols appeared on the streets of the major cities.

About the same time, a compromise between Walesa (who acted almost unilaterally) and the Government regarding workers' councils was reached. Walesa accepted the *Sejm*, not the union version. The Government was given the initiative to nominate managers of defense and some key industries, the workers controlling the others. Both parties were supposed to consult each other and had the right of court appeal in case of disagreement.

The Government was evidently satisfied with the arrangement, despite a last-ditch attempt to make the labor law sterner. But it then faced an open revolt of its own deputies and of others. However, the hotheads in Solidarity were angry, despite the fact that Parliament, during its debate, was in constant touch and consultation with the union. The Government's compliance made nothing of their plans for the national referendum.

To the majority of workers the question of councils was mostly that of indifference. Food and housing shortages, the tremendous lines in front of shops and their empty shelves, speculation and the exorbitant prices on the black market, inflation (the dollar had become almost the second currency of the Polish People's Republic) were immediate concerns; and after more than a year of Solidarity activities, the Party's reforms and purges had not brought the slightest improvement in the economic situation.

The Government was now in a conciliatory mood. Stefan Olszowski stated that Solidarity should have a formal part in Polish political life. Stanislaw Ciosek, the Minister in charge of trade unions, suggested a place for Solidarity in the National Unity Front. Jaruzelski coupled a stern warning to Solidarity with a plan to establish an advisory group for the Government composed of various social and trade union organizations. In a way, this was a counter-proposal to the suggestion of many Solidarity activists to reestablish the second chamber (i.e., Senate) or a "shadow cabinet" as an adjunct to the Premier's office.

Thus, an unprecedented phenomenon in post-war Poland reappeared—the process of political bargaining. What was lost at Teheran, Yalta, and Potsdam was being regained. The historic circle which started in 1939 with the war for Polish freedom was returning to its original point. Whether this tremendous opportunity would be recognized depended in great measure on the second part of the Solidarity conference, on the political maturity and acumen of the delegates.

The pious Walesa prayed, kneeling before the Congress that reconvened in Gdansk. The Polish anthem and "God Who Created Poland" were sung. Significantly, but perhaps not too wisely, many delegates' cars bore signs: "We are not afraid."

The sharpest dispute from the beginning centered on the new law for workers' self-management. Walesa was severely criticized for agreeing to the compromise at a meeting of only four members (out of ten) of the presidium.

Gwiazda stated that he was not even notified of the meeting, that he considered the decision to be a deplorable political mistake, and that the people responsible for it had been representing an army of ten million. At least a dozen delegates criticized the compromise as going too far, or as a betrayal of the union's democratic principles.

Walesa, visibly angered by his contumacious brethren, shouted that sometimes one had to behave like a dictator while dealing with concrete political situations. [Concerning dictatorship, Walesa said a few days later: ". . . there was dictatorship because there was no program, no statutes. But now we will have a program. So let us treat the earlier period more leniently" (*Los Angeles Times*, September 30, 1981, part I, p. 16)]. The new law gave the workers' councils a legal basis, and would help in their development. And ideas of destroying Parliament and the Government would lead to totalitarianism.

Evidently Walesa, in his year of official political activities, had grown in posture, while most of the Solidarity members remained at their previously low level of awareness of political realities.

Jan Rulewski contended that as long as Solidarity had no free access to the media and was being slandered, the search for compromise with the Government was meaningless. The union, according to him, was created not to compromise, but to smash the totalitarian system.

The next day, Edward Lipinski, the ninety-three year old nestor of

Polish socialism, announced dissolution of the KOR, whose main purpose was to defend workers and political activists victimized by the Government. With the emergence of a mass movement for democratic rights, the KOR had fulfilled its role. KOR's announcement ended on a pathetic note:

> We served the cause of Polish freedom and the cause of freedom of Poles in Poland as we could and as we knew, as dictated to us by our conscience and our understanding of the situation. Before our eyes we had the ideal of a Poland which was famed for tolerance and freedom, of a Poland which knew how to be the common fatherland of Poles, Bielo-Russians, Lithuanians, and Jews, the fatherland of all its citizens regardless of language, religion, and national origin.
>
> It is not for us to appraise our work. We wanted it to be our contribution to the great national undertaking, the creation of an independent, just, and democratic Poland. [*Tygodnik Solidarnosc* (Warsaw), October 9, 1981, p. 7, also as reported in the *Los Angeles Times*, September 28, 1981. Professor Lipinski said that he had been a socialist since 1906. According to Lipinski, socialism was to be the solution of the working class problem, the liberation of the working class, etc. But the socialism which was practiced in Poland was the socialism of mismanagement, bringing a catastrophe unequaled in the last two hundred years of Polish history. It was the socialism of prisons, censorship, and police which had been destroying Poland for thirty years.]

The next day brought a debate on the Solidarity program. By now Solidarity was to be not just a trade union, but a movement for social rebirth, the force behind the national revival, with a key role in almost all phases of Polish life. It was the sole guarantor of the 1980 Gdansk Accord, and, as such, recognized as its duty the initiation of long- and short-term actions to save the fatherland from collapse.

The final text of the program, which reads like a platform of a political party, was published as a supplement to number 29 of *Tygodnik Solidarnosc*, on October 16, 1981. It is tabloid in form and contains sixteen pages of small print. It says:

> We are an organization which unites characteristics of a trade union and of a great social movement. Consolidation of these features establishes the strength of our organization and decides our role in the life of the whole nation. Thanks to the creation of a powerful trade union organization, Polish society ceased to be atomized, disorganized, and lost. It has united under the call for solidarity and has recovered strength and hope. The conditions for the real national renaissance have been brought to life. Our union, the largest representation of working people in Poland, wants to be and will be the cause of this renaissance (*Tygodnik Solidarnosc* [Warsaw], October 16, 1981, p. 1).

Further on, the program gives thirty-seven theses on how to achieve economic reform and rebirth of the Republic—mainly through fighting bureaucracy, liquidation of command economy, workers' councils, increases in industrial production, and, significantly, through monetary reform and the raising of prices. The struggle against crisis and for reform must be done under society's control.   Political pluralism should be the basis for democracy in the Republic, which has to guarantee fundamental freedoms. The judiciary should be independent, etc.

This is a curious document, binding together elements of a political platform with an act which might be described as constitution-building, the very essence of politics. The program ends with a request for a new social contract.

Taken on the whole and in the context of Polish political and economic conditions, Solidarity's program offered a blueprint not for evolution but for revolution. Its Aesopic language was obvious, its threats clearly implied, and its demands made from a position of power.

There was the usual bow towards the Soviet Union, in the shape of assurances that sovereign Poland would remain in the Warsaw Pact. But given Solidarity's political immaturity and arrogance, how much trust could the Russians have in such a promise? They knew that the union was expressing deep feelings of Polish nationalism, and that the centuries-long hatred of Poland towards its imperialistic neighbor would not easily be dissipated.

Solidarity's great design might, perhaps, have worked on the island of Utopia, but not in the world as it is.

Treating the Party as an occupying power (an especially salient feature of the subsequent Radom Declaration) was not only an unnecessary provocation, but was an oversimplification which made an accord between the two impossible. With all its faults and errors, the Party is a native ruling elite shaped by its society and the forces of history, not a mere assemblage of Stalinistic stooges.

Also Solidarity, in spite of its heterogeneous nature, did not represent the whole nation, but only embodied long-term national aspirations for true independence. This was not a party of political realism, but of negation. The Polish national character, anarchistic but conforming, made impossible a compromise between moderates of all political hues and the ruling elite.

On October 2nd, the thirteenth day of the Solidarity Conference, more mundane matters of down-to-earth politics were settled. The question was, "who would be the Chairman of the National Coordinating Commission?" Walesa was opposed by three radicals: Marian Jurczyk, the head of the Solidarity chapter from Szczecin; Andrzej Gwiazda, the ideologue; and Jan Rulewski, of Bydgoszcz-incident fame. Walesa received 55.2 percent of the votes cast (462); Marian Jurczyk, 24.01 percent (201); Andrzej Gwiazda, 8.84 percent (74); and Jan Rulewski, only 6.21 percent (52). There were 844 votes, 7 of them invalid (*Tygodnik Solidarnosc* [Warsaw], October 8, 1981).

Thus, atypically for most revolutions, the forces of moderation won.

But there was an incident which radicalized labor opinion and almost started a Gdansk Tobacco Party. The Government chose the time of the conference to announce an increase in the prices of cigarettes and tobacco; and a very stormy session of the Congress ensued. The smokers, a majority among the delegates (it may be worth noting that Walesa himself is a chain smoker), were ready to call a general strike. This Government action caused a much stronger reaction than the recent tripling of bread prices. Lech Walesa sent a stern telegram to Jarulzelski, and immediately several Cabinet Ministers were dispatched to Gdansk. Gradually, the delegates calmed. The Government timing smacked of provocation or stupidity.

There were surprises in the election of the Solidarity Coordinating Commission. Some of Walesa's old friends and allies were defeated, such as Bronislaw Gieremek, Seweryn Jaworski, and Ryszard Bugaj.

Eventually the mammoth Congress ended on October 7, 1981. The delegates demanded, as parting shots, a freeze on further price increases, and the establishment of people's tribunals to punish the former officials who were responsible for the crisis. The leading role of the Party was neither denied nor affirmed. Solidarity was boldly declared to be a mass organization, a movement for national revitalization.

When the delegates at last dispersed, the 107-member National Commission elected its executive body. Most of them were new people, except for Janusz Onyszkiewicz and Grzegorz Palka, who reputedly were adherents to Walesa's relatively moderate policy, as were his two deputies, Stanislaw Wadolowski and Miroslaw Krupinski. The members of the commission became a shadow cabinet, on the British mode, taking various portfolios.

The Government continued various conciliatory approaches to Solidarity, but the union did not respond. The hardliners and Moscow were losing patience. The sacrificial goat had to be found.

On October 16-18 the IV Plenum of PUWP's Central Committee convened, and Stanislaw Kania, in spite of his anti-Solidarity speech, was removed from his post. On the recommendation of the Political Bureau he was replaced by General Wojciech Jaruzelski, who now had concentrated in his hands the three most important positions in the country: Defense Minister, Premier, and First Secretary of the Party. The IV Plenum also declared that Solidarity had broken the social contract, appealed for the end to strikes, and announced that, if necessary, the government would use its constitutional rights to defend the vital interests of the nation and state. But the union remained undaunted, and when the Deputy Prime Minister Mieczyslaw Rakowski proposed a mutual Solidarity-Government commission on the food crisis, the union refused to participate unless it would be allowed before the negotiations to present its views on television.

Meanwhile, thousands and thousands of workers had been striking to protest food shortages, and a general protest strike took place on

October 18. The government, to placate the strikers and Solidarity, froze food prices. The most amazing proposal to solve the crisis came from the semi-official group Experience and Future (DIP—*Doswiadczenie i Przvszlosc*), which suggested a coalition government! Such a government would enjoy the trust of a majority of the people, assumed the DIP, and lead Poland out of its mess. Of course, the key governmental positions would be reserved sanctimoniously for the Party. Nonetheless, a historical phase had come to an end. Since its inception in August, 1980 to Kania's downfall, in October 1981, Solidarity had changed the political norms in Poland, toppling two governments (two Secretaries of the Party), and influencing international politics. It had brought irrevocable alterations in Polish life and had become a de facto opposition party, an experiment unheard of in the Eastern bloc. The two centers of power were now a reality. This was a new situation for the Polish United Workers Party and the Soviet Union. Was it possible to accomplish anything more without wrecking the present achievements? The future of Poland, and perhaps much more, depended now on the political abilities and maturity of the Solidarity leadership.

And while there was still time for reflection, a significant event took place. The Government, allegedly to help food distribution, but certainly to check the dependency and discipline of the troops, sent small military detachments to villages. The soldiers spent about four weeks in the country and were then moved to the cities. This deployment of troops, and the simultaneous prolongation of military service for conscripts, were the first harbingers of martial law.

A communique issued around this time by the revitalized Front of National Unity, the organization of non-communist but servile parties, summed up the country's situation as follows: "The economy is disintegrating, the economic links between country and towns are disappearing. The vital interests of society, nation, and the state are threatened."

General Jaruzelski, in a desperate gesture, one perhaps frowned upon by the Kremlin, gave his imprimatur to the idea of coalition government, and as a token of good will, appointed some non-communists to the cabinet. But Solidarity was not impressed, and eschewed the proposal on the historically correct basis that in past such government moves were but a sham; it would be wrong, they said, for the union to grant such credibility, which at present was nil, to the disgraced rulers.

Parliament pleaded for an end to the wildcat strikes which were idling some 350,000 workers in mining and other key industries, and the presidium of Solidarity joined in that appeal. However, the executive leadership either was not sincere or had lost its influence over the mass membership; its exhortations (and those of Walesa's) had minimal effect. At the crucial time of Walesa's talks with General Jaruzelski and Archbishop Glemp, talks aimed at finding some *modus vivendi* for the full body of all the parties, the National Commission issued one of its ultimatums: if its demands were not accepted, " . . . the commission will seek the union members' support for the above demands by a statutory action throughout all of Poland, a general strike included" (*Tygodnik Solidarnosc*, [Warsaw], November 13, 1981, p. 3), to which, however, the Presidium added a rider that, ". . . the Presidium of the National Commission confirms that in any negotiations with the government, the N.C. is and will be ready for a compromise based on the supreme welfare of the whole Polish Society" (Ibid.). Nevertheless, the National Commission offered the government a revolutionary program in a nutshell, as its demands requested: a powerful Social Council of National Economy (Spoleczna Rada Gospodarki Narodowej), independent of and capable of censuring the government, consisting mainly of Solidarity trustees; reform of the economy to make the workers' councils its basic units; full access to the mass media (mainly radio and television); democratization of local government; reform of the legal system and of the price structure.

On November 11th, the anniversary of Poland's proclamation of independence in 1918 was broadly celebrated throughout Poland, with quasi-participation of the government. The Solidarity weekly printed on its first page Marshal Pilsudski's 1918 telegram to world governments in which he had announced the rebirth of the Polish state. The Marshal's portraits were displayed and sold everywhere, to the great chagrin of the Russians, to whom Pilsudski was anathema. In Warsaw thousands took part in a Mass, march, and rally. Symbolically, scouts led the parade, followed by veterans of the first world war, of the anti-Bolshevik war, and World War II. Very noticeable were large contingents of Solidarity, and members of the Confederation for Independent Poland (KPN).

The Government-Solidarity talks started at last, but the union, seemingly acting from a position of power, requested further democratization, pluralism in political life, and a real partnership between union and government, stating: " . . .The now existing political institutions, which were supposed to be the vehicle for national unity, with the obsolete sham Front of National Unity (Front Jednosci Narodowej) at their head, cannot fulfill such tasks . . . We think that we should start building an accord not from the roof down but from the foundations up" (*Tygodnik Solidarnosc,* [Warsaw], November 27, 1981).

Meanwhile, Lech Walesa, in a stroke of genius, solved the Polish food crisis by appealing to the working people of Western Europe to pressure their governments to feed Poland throughout the winter. But before the capitalistic states could oblige, an unheard of event took place in Poland, once the land of milk and honey, once the bread basket of Europe—food riots broke out in which shopkeepers and grocery clerks were killed. Now the clerks threatened to strike. Anarchy had come full circle, with strikes being planned against strikes. The black market and speculation thrived. The peasants, as during the Occupation, refused government money for their products, requesting instead payment in hard currencies or in gold and jewelry.

General Jaruzelski announced that the Party was preparing a draft of anti-strike legislation to be pushed through the Parliament, the only alternative to "a war-type state." At the same time, he wooed Solidarity to the Front of National Accord, leaking word that otherwise there would be a confrontation. In many parts of Poland physical confrontations between the government and Solidarity and its sympathizers were already taking place, sometimes provoked by the government, sometimes by the union. The most publicized of these was the sit-in in Warsaw by cadet firemen, who were forcibly removed by militia and crack troops in a SWAT-like operation. During that incident, Solidarity's workers' militia made its appearance, while the government revitalized the official workers' militia (SR). All these events were taking place against the background of perennial strikes, semi-strikes, and warning strikes, which included now farmers, students, and even, allegedly, schoolchildren.

In this impasse the national executive of Solidarity met with the regional leaders in Radom. Purposefully and significantly, Radom was chosen as it was the scene of the past brutal beatings of unionists, and of a present conflict over the rectorship of the polytechnic college.

The Solidarity conference place was either bugged, or one of the unionists was receiving Government pay, as the authorities obtained "Radomgate" tapes, making them public on television, radio, and in the press. The recording quality was bad, the voices indistinct. Some sentences were obviously taken out of context, and some words cannot be taken literally; the meaning of others is unclear. But altogether, they are still surprisingly revealing. Lech Walesa was heard saying:

"...Confrontation is unavoidable and will take place. People should realize it right now. I wanted to reach that confrontation in a natural way, where practically all social groups would be with us; but I have miscalculated...We would then overthrow the *Sejm* (Parliament), councils, and so forth. It seems that we are no longer progressing with these tactics. Therefore, we are choosing a road with a view of making a lightning maneuver. Either with me or without me....It is clear that Gwiazda ceased to be a member of the executive not because our aims differ; we differed only in that his way and that of Jan (Rulewski?) require tanks, airplanes, and other things to be taken at once . . . We could have started shouting loudly and organized another November insurrection (1831) and called for scythes. This would surely look very pretty but we would lose . . ."

It appears that Walesa means by the word "confrontation" a general strike. Jacek Kuron said: "The issue of elections and a new electoral law, total negation of the so-called provisional pre-reform system, and the state of emergency, should become the field for confrontation. The ground must be prepared now by actions designed to overpower the authorities." Jan Rulewski: " . . . The provisional government will stabilize the country. It will be non-party government. It should follow KOR tactics (Committee for Social Self-defense), and not that of KPN (Confederation for Independent Poland), tactics based on over-taking, inhibiting, and exposing moves by the party." Grzegorz Palka: " . . . The Party can delay the confrontation, because it has the power, and "Solidarnosc" (Solidarity) lacks such power. Therefore, we have to create workers' militia which will be armed with helmets and batons." Zbigniew Bujak: " . . The first action of the workers' militia will be aimed at the liberation of radio and television headquarters. The social council for national economy must be established immed-iately. It will be something like a provisional government. The govern-ment must be at last overthrown, laid bare, and stripped of all credi-bility." Seweryn Jaworski to Walesa: " . . . if you retreat even one step, I will myself cut your head off; and if I don't, someone else will . . ." Due to popular demand—and no doubt there was one—the recording was repeated frequently on radio and TV, and printed in newspapers.

But the overwhelming question in the public mind was whether or not the tapes were authentic. Solidarity press spokesman, Marek Brunno, did not deny their genuineness. Neither did the weekly *Solidarnosc*, though it did express its horror at Watergate-style methods, and re-minded the Party of Nixon's fate.

Evidently Solidarity regarded as more important the so-called Radom stance, published in its weekly newspaper and various other publi-cations, a document which later became known as the "Radom De-claration." This stated that the government surprised the union by introducing through its Party deputies parliamentary legislation on principles of business operations in 1982 (the "provisory arrange-ment"—*prowizorium systemowe*), legislation which was contrary to the interests of the working people. Also, the document said that, should Parliament pass a law giving the government extraordinary powers, there would be a 24-hour protest strike; and, if the government dared to use those powers, there would be a general strike. Radom also accused the government of using the talks on national accord as a screen to cover preparations for an attack on the union: "In this situation, further negotiations on the subject of the national accord are irrele-vant" (*Tygodnik Solidarnosc*, [Warsaw], November 11, 1981).

The union further demanded halting of anti-Solidarity activities; independent workers' councils; withdrawal of "provisory arrange-ments"; democratic elections for the regional councils (Rady Wojewodz-kie); establishment of a Socio-Economic Council; and free access to radio and television for itself, the Church, and other groups. "These are the minimal conditions for a national accord which will make possible an effective fight against the crisis. We will vote for such agreement" (Ibid.).

On December 11, the Solidarity National Commission convened at the Lenin Shipyard in Gdansk to debate officially over the government proposal for a Front of National Accord. The mood of the speakers was markedly radical. Jan Rulewski suggested a provisional government by experts, and free elections to Parliament if the Government would not implement the peoples' demands. According to Jerzy Kropownicki, national accord was impossible because the Party was to be one of the partners. Seweryn Jaworski called for Solidarity workers' militia over the entire country. The voice of moderation was represented by the lawyer Wladyslaw Sila Nowicki, the man accused (voice indistinct) in "Radomgate" of a desire to send all the Communists to the gallows. According to him, the government was not seeking a confrontation, neither was Solidarity, though it gave this impression through clumsy formulations about workers' militia, street demonstrations, and the Radom Declaration.

Equally important as the growing radicalization of the National Commission was that of Lech Walesa, who in a statement given to the Warsaw daily, *Zycie Warszawy*, rather equivocally said that the radicals had been right all along. His only difference from them was that he wanted to achieve the same goals without a fist fight. According to the AFP press agency, Walesa said at the meeting in Gdansk that he wanted to seek an *entente* to drag things out, if necessary, to spring, before coming to a broad political solution. But he realized at Radom that it was impossible to wait any longer.

During the second day of the debates, the speakers were no less radical than previously. The prevailing theme was that the people could no longer tolerate the anti-democratic and incompetent government. Thus, the nation should mobilize around the Radom Declaration, which should in turn become a subject of referendum. A provisional government and free elections were suggested, along with so-called "active strikes," i.e., the taking over of production and distribution by the workers. A number of resolutions were passed, of which details are not available. However, the two most important resolutions were made public. The National Commission formally approved a general strike if the *Sejm* adopted the legislation giving extraordinary powers to the government; and the Radom Declaration became the official position of the union and hopefully of the entire nation.

For Jaruzelski, this was the final challenge to communist rule in Poland. The day was December 12, 1981, the last day of the Independent, Self-Governing Trade Union Solidarity.

At midnight, a state of war (emergency) was declared and martial law imposed. Solidarity was suspended and its leaders arrested. The army took over. Said General Wojciech Jaruzelski:

> Citizens of the Polish People's Republic, I turn to you as a soldier, and as the head of the Polish Government. I speak to you about matters of utmost importance. Our country has found itself on the brink of a precipice.

The achievement of many generations, the house built on Polish ashes, is being destroyed. The mechanism of state is ceasing to function. New blows are falling on the dying economy. The present living conditions impose increasingly difficult burdens on our people. Lines of painful divisions run through many Polish homes. The atmosphere of endless conflicts, of misunderstanding and hatred, is causing psychological damage, and injures our tradition of tolerance. Strikes, strike readiness, and protest actions have become the norm . . . The nation has come to the end of its psychological endurance . . . the national economy has been turned into an arena of political struggle. A deliberate torpedoing of government activities has brought about a situation where the results are not commensurate with our efforts. We did not lack good will, moderation, and patience. Perhaps there was even too much of it sometimes. It is hard to fail to notice the respect for the social agreement shown by the government. We have gone even further. The initiative for the great national accord won the support of millions of Poles. It created an opportunity for the democratic system to be rooted more deeply, and for the range of reforms to be broader. These hopes were frustrated. The Solidarity leadership was not present at the conference table. The words spoken in Radom and during the session in Gdansk revealed their true intentions. These intentions are confirmed on a mass scale by every-day practice, by the increasing militancy of the extremists, by an open striving for the partition of the socialist Polish state. How long can one wait for a sobering-up? How long can a hand extended for agreement be met with a fist? I say this with a burdened heart and immense bitterness. Things could have been different. They should be different. The continuation of the present state of affairs would inevitably lead to a catastrophe, to complete chaos and famine . . .

The nation's instinct for self-preservation must win. Adventurists must have their hands bound before they would push the fatherland into the abyss of fratricide . . .

Citizens, great is the burden of responsibility which falls on me at this dramatic moment in Polish history. It is my duty to take this responsibility. Poland's future is at stake . . .

I announce that today the Military Council of National Salvation is established. The Council of State in accordance with the constitution, introduced today at midnight a state of war [emergency] throughout the country. I wish everyone to understand the motives and aims of our action. We are not attempting a military coup, a military dictatorship. The nation has enough strength, enough wisdom to develop by itself an efficient system of socialistic rule. In such a system the army will remain where it should be—in the barracks. No Polish problem in the long run can be solved by force. The Military Council for National Salvation is not replacing the constitutional organs of power. Its sole role is the protection of legal order, and the creation of an executive guarantee which will make it possible to restore order and discipline . . .

The Military Council will be dissolved when the rule of law once again reigns, when conditions permit the normal functioning of the civil administration and of representative bodies . . .

Citizens—just as there is no turning back from socialism, so there is no turning back to the erroneous methods and practices of pre-August,

1980 . . . All important reforms will be continued . . .

We are a sovereign country and must emerge from this crisis on our own. It is with our hands that we remove the threat . . . Poland is and will remain a permanent link in the Warsaw treaty, and an unfailing member of the socialist community of nations . . .

Let us together for our own good remove the specter of civil war. Let us not build barricades where bridges are necessary . . . Give up for the fatherland your inalienable right for strike for as long as it may be necessary to overcome the greatest of difficulties . . .

The Military Council proclaimed that it would act through departmental, voievodship, municipal, parish plenipotentiaries, and commissars of the committee for the country's defense. Railroads, ports, transportation, communication, fire departments, and power plants were "militarized," and their workers became subject to wartime discipline. Strikes were forbidden and a curfew announced. Schools and universities were closed and public meetings banned. The army and militia were authorized to use firearms and all means of enforcement to ensure peace and order. Among other things, the Military Council declared: "The conditions of martial law make it necessary to suspend the activities of trade unions."

That sentence more than other sounded the official death knell for Solidarity. It had lasted for only 469 days, a period filled with significance for the future of communism in Eastern Europe, an era whose effects on history may continue for decades to come. With its mixture of clericalism and nationalism, Solidarity was not the pure workers' party of the utopian Marxist future, nor was it a wholly democratic party in the American style. In some respects it is a measure of Marx's victory from the grave that Solidarity achieved international recognition and support as a labor union, not simply as a nationalistic movement for political, social, or economic independence. For historians and political scientists, the Solidarity phenomenon will be, perhaps, primarily a precedent-setting textbook case of *a revolution which nearly succeeded, a grassroots uprising instigated by a generation of ordinary people born and raised under the communist system*. Whether or not the Solidarity movement is the first sign of a major transformation of the Soviet-led bloc, or whether it is just one in a long series of popular revolts squelched by men who can tolerate no dissidence, remains to be seen. For the first time in the history of postwar Europe, however, a communist-controlled government has failed so abyssmally in managing its own affairs that the military has been forced to take control. Another significant factor is that the Soviet Union failed to take direct action, despite extreme provocation from its point of view. No longer are decisions of state in Eastern Europe a simple matter of heel grinding.

Chapter 3

What Is To Be Done?
The Burden of the Past
and the Threat of the Future

The troubles in Poland may be understood without any special knowledge of the peculiarities of Polish national character or the history of that country. Conclusions derived from the recent events in Poland have universal applications, but some broad background material may give coherence to the reader's impressions.

The roots of this conflict are to be found more than a millennium ago, when the Polish King Mieszko I decided to accept the Western version of Christianity through the good services of his Czech brethren, and, to seal the bargain, offered (through an act called *Dagome iudex*) to put Poland under Rome's protection. Thus, Poland remained Catholic when most of the Slav states around it became Orthodox; Poland was the Eastern outpost of Western civilization, involved in endless wars with Tartars, Turks, Protestants, Orthodox Russians, and Ukrainians.

The same roots may be seen in the decision of the Russian ruler, Vladimir the Great, who about a quarter of a century later decided to accept Orthodox Christianity from Byzantium (or Constantinople). Since then, the cultural, religious, and political development of these two great Slav nations have moved along different roads.

What has followed is a long, rich, and colorful history, full of great moments; unfortunately, in the process, Poland went from the position of being the largest and most powerful monarchy in Europe to a state of anarchical "squire democracy," which ultimately led to three partitions in the latter part of the eighteenth century, wherein Russia was the chief culprit.

The last of these partitions extinguished Poland as a state until the year 1918, and also upset the European balance of power, with consequences lasting up to this very moment. During the intervening century, "Poland" became an integral part of the Russian empire. Poland regained her independence after World War I, only to be partitioned again in 1939 with the infamous Ribbentrop-Molotov pact. During the Second World War, Poland's underground resistance flourished; the exiled portions of its armed forces fought the Germans alongside the Western Allies, suffering enormous casualties. In 1944 an uprising took place in Warsaw, directed physically against the Germans, but politically against the Russians. The Russians were already on the other shore of the Vistula, and had occupied half of Poland, where they created a puppet government. In the unequal struggle, Warsaw was completely destroyed and its population dispersed, either taken to Germany or to concentration camps. The Russians, obviously, not only did not help the uprising, but forbade the reloading of British and American planes on the other bank of the Vistula.

By secret treaties in Teheran and at Yalta, Poland was not so much sold to Russia as given away as a present. A face-saving gesture was made by the Western Allies, who requested democratic government and free elections.

Stalin had no objection to the promise, but plenty of objection to its realization. In a bloody but short civil war, in which Wladyslaw Gomulka played a prominent role, and in which Jaruzelski was one of the generals fighting the armed opposition, the Polish communist regular forces, supported by Russians, won. The only official opposition group allowed was the Peasants' Party, under an ex-*emigre* politician, Stanislaw Mikolajczyk, which was quickly and brutally destroyed. Stalinism was introduced and lasted until the so-called October Revolution of 1956. Trade unions became the obedient tools of the Party.

In 1956 events happened which were a prelude to the Solidarity renewal or *odnowa*. At that time the chain of command from the Kremlin broke down while the Soviet rulers were busily engaged in settling their own accounts. Stalin's protege, Boleslaw Bierut, Poland's President and the First Secretary of the Party, suddenly died. He was replaced by Edward Ochab, a Khrushchev protege. Meanwhile, Nikita's famous speech on Stalinism was made known in the Party's circles, and de-Stalinization began.

The Party apparatus was disorganized. The leaders did not know which faction in Moscow would emerge victorious from the struggle for power, or, consequently, whose instructions should be obeyed. A power struggle began in the Polish United Workers' Party. Suddenly, some past errors were discovered, and the guilty ones pointed out. Censorship became disoriented. Bold articles appeared. Everywhere there were mass Party and non-Party meetings. People began talking with less fear. New organizations, and even embryonic political parties, were mushrooming. The huge one-million-member communist youth organization, Zwiazek Mlodziezy Polskiej (ZMP), was dissolved, the first step toward separating the integrated Socialist Party and

Communist Party, which had been joined together under the heading of the United Workers' Party in 1948.

But in spite of all the changes, the mechanism of Party apparatus was intact. There was no alternative organization, such as was created almost a quarter century later by Solidarity. The reform movement was filtered and channelled by the Party. The changes had personal, not systemic, character, especially when numerous old Stalinists suddenly discovered the error of their ways and joined, or tried to join, the current group. The low and middle echelons of the Party requested a return to pure communism unspoiled by "a cult of personality," a popular euphemism for Stalin's cult. Actually, the unversed masses were not quite sure whether the "cult of the individual" or of "personality" referred to Stalin, Bierut, or perhaps someone else.

The low Party members and the population at large requested the return of Gomulka, who had been removed by Stalin because of a difference in their views on collectivization of Polish agriculture. For a short while, Gomulka (who was once imprisoned for his political views— a most certain way of gaining popularity in Poland), was as admired as was Walesa in August of 1980, or perhaps Cardinal Wyszynski.

Wladyslaw Gomulka regained power without the slightest effort on his part. He rode on the wave, as Walesa did later. Gomulka was simply available. To the popular mind, he was a nationalist hero who had dared to oppose Stalin in his attempt at further Sovietization of Poland. Besides, the man who went to prison because of his politics evidently was not an opportunist.

But from the system's point of view, the all-important factor was that Gomulka was a Party man. There was not, and could not be allowed, any alternative structure to convey and express potentially destructive demands.

There was popular request for change, and the political climate altered. Thousands of political prisoners were released, and tens of thousands of Poles who had been deported by Stalin to Soviet Russia were repatriated. More importantly, while the Party apparatus remained intact, the terror apparatus was partially dismantled. Stalin's henchmen, Stanislaw Radkiewicz and Jakub Berman of Internal Security, were removed from their posts. The two most notoriously sadistic Officers of Security, Roman Romkowski and Anatol Fejgin, were put on trial, and hundreds of lesser fish sacked. Another of Stalin's men, Hilary Minc, resigned from the Politbureau and from his post as Minister of Economy.

As previously mentioned, the climate of political opinion changed, and there was spontaneous socialization. But the same old rulers were in control; they thought that by bringing back Gomulka, who was being rehabilitated like thousands of other people, both communists and non-communists, the populace would be mollified. Such probably would have been the course of events if not for the occurrence which became the precedent for the events leading up to the Gdansk Accord in 1980 and the appearance of Solidarity.

On June 28, 1956 riots, basically economic in origin, erupted in Poznan. The Government called in troops and tanks, and a battle with the population ensued. Telephone communications were cut off, but secrecy was impossible to maintain, because the events took place during the International Trade Fair, and foreigners and foreign journalists filled the town.

Jozef Cyrankiewicz, the iron Premier who had managed to survive almost all the regimes in postwar Poland, announced that the hand who dared to threaten socialism would be severed. The riots were blamed on imperialists and Radio Free Europe.

But soon a pattern was established that would continue to the present day. Edward Ochab, speaking to a Party Plenum, said that the riots were, after all, not caused by foreign imperialists, but were a tragedy which happened because the Party was not aware of the actual situation and mood in the country.

The climax came in October of 1956. Previously, Gomulka had been readmitted to the Party and his allies given some key jobs; notably, Waclaw Komar was Chief of the Internal Security Corps (KBW), the crack, well-equipped troops arranged on a military mode.

The Party members vociferously demanded Gomulka's return to ultimate power, and most of the population enthusiastically agreed. Gomulka was to be the answer to all Polish problems. [When this writer opposed Gomulka on the grounds of his past activities *vis-a-vis* the Polish anti-communist resistance, his treatment of the Home Army (Armia Krajowa), and his demolition of Mikolajczyk's Peasants' Party (PSL), he was accused of being a direct Soviet agent or Piasecki's pro-Soviet agent.] The country was not in chaos, but merely in flux.

The events which actually led to Gomulka's return are not yet clear. The following version is based partly on knowledge gained through the author's personal participation and role in the so-called October Revolution of 1956, and on various articles in the Polish and *emigre* press, but mainly on accounts in *Kultura* (Paris) and *Nowe Drogi* (Warsaw).

The Party Plenum was due to convene on October 18, 1956. There was popular gossip that the so-called "Natolin Group" of hardline Stalinists was preparing a *coup d'etat*. The Soviet troops stationed in Silesia, in the west of Poland, were moving towards Warsaw, as were the Soviet units to the east. In the capital there was excitement, colossal mass meetings at public squares and halls, and marches along the main streets, where anti-Soviet slogans were shouted and Gomulka and Cardinal Wyszynski (the odd couple) were appealed to for deliverance. It was then that I heard for the first time in my life a public request for Poland's sovereignty. Fortunately or unfortunately, the Soviet Embassy, an original target of many marches, was spared.

It was rumored that the Soviet ruling clique had arrived at the Plenum, namely Khrushchev, Molotov, Kaganovich, and Konev. What was only gossiped in the streets became official news when Ochab greeted the Soviet dignitaries, and then proposed including in the CC Wladyslaw Gomulka, plus Zenon Kliszko, Marian Spychalski, and Ignacy Loga-Sowinski, all of them old Gomulka supporters. The motion was carried and made public.

Gomulka, together with the whole membership of the Politbureau, went to Belveder, the presidential palace, for talks with the uninvited Soviet guests. Khrushchev and company were deeply disturbed about the threat to the socialist system in Poland, and the possibility of a break in Polish-Soviet relations, with a subsequent Polish withdrawal from the Warsaw Pact.

Somehow Gomulka was able to convince the Soviet delegation of his servility to Moscow. However, nobody knew it as yet, and the situation was tense. It was rumored that Soviet tanks had tried to enter the Varsavian outskirts, and were stopped by Komar's Internal Security Corps.

The Polish army was still nominally under the command of the Soviet Marshal, Konstantin Rokossovskii, but under de facto command of Spychalski and other Polish generals. The Russian advisers and specialists, as well as the Russian officers in Polish uniforms, were quietly and unobtrusively isolated. The movements of the Soviet troops were reported by the Polish Army to the CC. In many factories the workers requested distribution of arms, and in many places the building of barricades was proposed or even started. Most of the events had a spontaneous character.

The Soviet guests, armed and unarmed, departed in peace, leaving their comrade, "Wieslaw" Gomulka, in the seat of power. In his speech at the Plenum, Gomulka sounded a by now familiar note:

> . . . Recently the working class gave a painful lesson to the party leadership and government. The workers of Poznan made use of the strike weapon and came out on the streets . . . . Workers of Poznan were not protesting against socialism or People's Poland . . . . They were in protest against the evils that spread so widely in our social system and which hurt them so painfully, and against distortions of the basic rules of socialism, which is their ideal....(*Nowe Drogi*, [Warsaw] October, 1956, with other sources).

Gomulka was now ruling Poland. It is not within the scope of this work to analyze his character or his rule; but it must be mentioned that Gomulka was not dishonest. His future behavior was easy to foretell for anyone who took the trouble to check his past record and who listened carefully to his speeches and announcements. He was also not a crazed, homocidal maniac of Stalin's ilk.

As soon as Gomulka held the reins of state, he put a damper on the October revolution. One of his first moves was to close the independent student papers. [Among the other publications, my own literary magazine, *Wspolczesnosc*, was shut down.] A year later he liquidated the famous *Po Prostu* weekly. Student demonstrations were denounced as hooliganism, and put down with the help of special riot militia and the so-called workers' militia (ORMO). Gradually, most of the October Revolution's achievements were recinded. The radicals who helped bring Gomulka back were isolated, and the obedient Stalinists taken back into service. The opportune moment was lost because there was no alternative structure or workers'-intellectuals' cooperation.

Gomulka's years in power were uneventful. Some economic reforms were introduced. Agriculture (i.e., peasants) was helped. The workers' council (the pet project, not only of Hannah Arendt in the West, but of the *Po Prostu* group in Poland) was domesticated and then sent into oblivion. Harrassment of small business and tradesmen, however, was stopped. Intellectuals were persecuted. The economic situation of the country improved, but the standard of living remained one of the lowest in Europe.

Early in 1968 a play, *Forefathers* (*Dziady*), by the Polish romantic poet Adam Mickiewicz (1798-1855), was staged. It was full of anti-Russian slogans applauded by the audiences. The play was banned. The students staged demonstrations demanding cultural and political freedom. The workers remained indifferent. Prague fever did not erupt in Poland. The students were beaten down and arrested. Then, in the wake of the Israeli-Egyptian war, there was a purge of Jews. It is difficult to judge whether the old device of anti-Semitism was used to distract attention from the Prague events and the students' demonstrations, or whether it was engineered against Gomulka (who had a Jewish wife) by General Moczar or even Gierek.

In 1970 Gomulka decided to revise production norms and to raise food prices. Workers of the Gdansk Lenin's Shipyard protested and marched on Party headquarters, the Security Office and other offices were raided, and records destroyed. The same events were repeated in Szczecin.

Prime Minister Jozef Cyrankiewicz duplicated his Poznan performance: events in the Baltic ports, he said, were being wrought by hooligans and imperialist agents. However, the Politbureau had a different opinion. Comrade "Wieslaw" Gomulka and his closest collaborators were removed from their posts. Edward Gierek became First Secretary.

Gierek had spent his youth in France and Belgium, where he was active in the local communist parties. He actively supported the Polish communist regime, and, on his return, was rewarded with a job in the Party apparatus. He advanced steadily, became a member of the Politbureau, and First Secretary in the mining district of Silesia. His reputation was that of a very good administrator, a technocrat.

When the new First Secretary of the Party addressed the nation on television and radio, he almost repeated verbatim the words of his predecessor about Poznan. The Party had to preserve close links with the workers. The strikers were absolved of any fault, since they had acted from honest motives.

Gierek entered onto the path of his "economic miracle." Some raises were given immediately to the strikers; others received them later. Gierek applied to the West for credit, which was given willingly, almost eagerly, and began investing heavily in industry, hoping to earn through future exports hard currency for the repayment of the debts. Agriculture was neglected. Everything went well in the beginning; people had money, consumer goods were imported, food was sufficient. But the global recession brought about mainly by OPEC also affected Poland, and the interest on the loans had to be paid.

It was time to return to more realistic economic policies. Socialist Poland was living in capitalist style, on credit; and capitalism was undergoing one of its downward business cycles. Gierek announced hikes in food prices. The workers struck again. The Gdansk Accord was signed, and a second government (i.e., the First Secretary) had been brought down by the holy power of the proletariat. It should be mentioned at this point that changes of First Secretaries of the Party in the communist system are much more significant than any changes in official Government positions, which are often relatively powerless figurehead titles.

This short history should provide sufficient background information to make possible a search for an explanation of the events which led to the unique political phenomenon of Solidarity, and to attempt some prognoses.

The primary cause for disruption was Stalin's death. Iosif Vissarionovich Dzhugashvili (Stalin's real name) was able to achieve and maintain an approximation of a closed system. He did this by isolating the Soviet Union and her satellites from the global system, by eliminating his opponents and potential enemies, and through the atomization of society. During his life, Poland was not so much a satellite as the frontier province of the Imperium. All loyalty went to Stalin. The Polish rulers were either personally chosen by him or at least affirmed. Even the head of the Polish army was Soviet Marshal Rokossovskii. Key posts, especially in the army and internal security, were in Russian hands. The Russians instigated a blatant policy of Sovietization, similar in many respects to that followed by the 19th-century tsarist regime. Just as Roman Catholics could feel at home in any other Catholic country, especially in church, so any Russian could feel almost at home in Poland, now made into a miniature Polish Russia.

When Stalin died, Lavrentii Beria was unable to inherit Stalin's power, and the ex-obedient Stalin-servant, Nikita Khrushchev, gained the upper hand. Khrushchev deStalinized the system as much as was necessary to impose his own personal rule. But the brief period of fratricidal struggle in the Kremlin cost the Imperium dearly in long-range effects, on many different fronts. Outside its direct sphere of activity, the communist world was soundly shaken. Mistakes which cost millions of human lives could not be glossed over as easily in the West as in Soviet Russia. The Hungarian Revolution of 1956 was another shock, even for true believers. Inside the satellites there were qualitative changes. Gomulka was outwardly subservient to Moscow, but was never its tool. Poland now had its own subsystem centered on Gomulka, a power center which was not simply a part of the larger Soviet system.

Gomulka was a lesser version of Stalin, without that man's Attila-Genghis Khan-Hitler qualities. He paid homage to Russia, believed the same religion, but was "lord" of his own fiefdom—that is, until the Baltic coast rebellion crushed him.

Gierek had none of his predecessor's original legitimacy or support. And, very much like some Third World leaders, he carried on successfully as long as there were foreign loans upon which to depend. But the measure of his independence in foreign affairs was that he was allowed by the Soviets to incur such huge debts in the first place, debts which had cumulated to such huge totals by 1982 that they threaten the economic structure of the entire Soviet system in Eastern Europe.

Gierek was put down in the same rough manner that Gomulka was; but there were great differences in the external and internal situations. This was 1980, and the difference was not just chronological. The passing years since 1945 had brought about the complete political regeneration of the nation and a significant change in its psychological climate.

In 1945 the majority of the population was comprised of old people and women with children. Millions of men had died in the war; other millions remained abroad; more tens of thousands were killed by the communists after the war. Those men who survived were either peasants, or, with many honorable exceptions, opportunists.

The country was in ruins, with its capital destroyed more completely than Hiroshima or Nagasaki; almost one-third of its eastern agricultural territories were taken away by Russia. In exchange, Poland had received from Germany its western territories, from which all the industrial machinery had been appropriated by the Soviet Union, and from where the native Germans had to be expelled in the greatest ethnographic shift of modern times. All attempts at political opposition were quickly and ruthlessly eliminated. The only opposition power left was the Catholic Church, but it was persecuted and its economic power broken.

In 1980 the new generation accounted for the majority of the population, with its normal proportion of males. These young people had not experienced war, and if they remembered the Stalinist terror, it was but vaguely. The apparatus of terror had been partially dismantled by Gomulka, and almost totally by Gierek. Cultural links with the West were reestablished and the Polish tradition was revived. The Polish people are very conscious of history; all the national insurrections against the Russians, together with a century of direct occupation by the Russians of a greater part of Poland, were now vividly remembered. Hatred for Russians and Russia became almost pathological.

At the same time, the Church was gaining influence. Official persecution and harrassment were light enough to give the Catholics the aureola of martyrdom without effectively hurting them. Even at the height of the Stalinist terror, it was claimed that Poland boasted more Catholic publications than Francoist Spain. A new breed of well-educated and politicized priests entered the stage.

Thus, paradoxically, in communist Poland the Church not only survived but was strengthened, and became a de facto partner in the political dialogue. As all other elements of political opposition were silenced, it became a magnet for opposition, and the representative and protector of the populace. One could protest officially the communist dogma only at the cost of accepting the Catholic ones.

Consequently clericalism permeated life in Poland. Lech Walesa was often seen in an entourage of black-frocked priests; he prayed and knelt in public places; in his buttonhole he displayed a miniature of the Holy Virgin from Czestochowa. He visited the Pope and cardinals. The delegates of the Solidarity Gdansk Conference piously attended the Mass, etc.

Another paradoxical situation emerged. The Church had once protected the people from the regime, giving them support and psychological asylum. Now Walesa was in a position to repay the debt. Unsolicited, he gained a radio Mass and various benefits for the Church. But in the monopolistic communist system in Poland, where the regime was the guarantor of favorable Church status quo, the only dialogue possible was between the Church and the Party. In the new situation of political plurality, the Church lost part of its power base and its monopolistic hold on opposition, coming into conflict with the KOR.

So the change of generations was one of the reasons for Gierek's downfall and Solidarity's appearance. The situation is not without numerous historical precedences, starting with the Confederation of Bar insurrection in 1768, and the introduction of the Third May Constitution in 1782. The line of division between realism and romanticism goes through the insurrections of 1794, 1831, and 1863, up through the Dmowski/Pilsudski conflict and the regaining of independence in 1918.

Many social scientists claim that history does not repeat itself. But in Poland the basic ingredients seem to change but little with each crisis. There is today the same central geographic position, the same overpowering imperialistic neighbor, the same idealistic young people who hate the Russians and think that they will be able to gain national sovereignty themselves, by force of arms if necessary.

The above potent mixture is the genesis of the present "troubles in

Poland," but could not have proceeded if the ruling elite had not failed miserably in maintaining their system. They did not reestablish control over the mechanism of terror, and fell short in communication and recruitment. Their failures resulted also from the worsening global economic situation, over-population, unemployment, and the growing expectation gap. Further, the system itself forced them to work in a very rigid ideological frame, leaving few options, even to those imaginative enough to see them.

The Party was not able to impress their system of values on society. To the contrary, the values remained the same "old fashioned" ones that had always collided with official goals and ideals.

There were also problems with the leaders at the top. Gierek, like his predecessors, did not realize the depth of popular resentment against communism and the total bankruptcy of its ideals [To the popular Polish mind, socialism is equal to communism, and communism to the Soviet version; Poles see no distinctions between any of them], and against domination by Russia. Russia was now hated doubly—for being Russia, and for its ideology. In the economic and managerial fields, there were lesser, but also significant lacunae in communication. Input on problems was not transposed into appropriate corrective measures, and critics, even among Party members, were punished for their concern.

Party recruitment was not succeeding. The Party was never strong numerically, and most of those who joined its ranks were opportunists. In economy, however, a new managerial class was created. These managers were members of the elite but not experts, as the nominations to most of the important positions were made not according to the abilities and qualifications of the candidates, but in accordance with the Party Rules (*nomenklatura*). Thus, people without proper education were appointed to leading roles in the complex and overpopulated industrial state.

In the field of communication, the requirements of Marxist-Leninist orthodoxy forced the regime to exalt the virtues of egalitarianism and other lofty communist ideals. The masses of population, though staunchly anti-communist, somehow thought the earthly paradise promised by Marx and his followers was their due. The gap between rising expectations and their realization was growing wider, especially when conditions of life in the West were no longer a secret. The Party became a hated "father figure." The Party had appropriated the leading role in the nation and as a result was blamed and held responsible for all its ills. The advantages of the system were hardly noticed.

The new elite, while professing hypocritically the communist egalitarian ideals, requested and received the privileges of rank. The contradictions between reality and the ideal could not be explained away by the whole gamut of Marxian scholasticism. Consequently, the situation was similar to that before the Reformation, though Walesa should not be compared to Luther. Socialization brought effects contrary to the Party's expectations. Socialism produced its own toxins.

The ruling elite were not in a position to rule efficiently or ruthlessly. Its power nucleus, the Party, was neither able nor willing to articulate and aggregate society's demands, and its rule-making and governing abilities were faulty. The system was out of equilibrium, and the toppling of the elite overdue.

This is a typical prerevolutionary situation, a particularly interesting phenomenon, as it shows that such prerevolutionary communalities can exist independently of the economic and political systems of the state.

The trends included: a financial and economic crisis of the state, the emergence of the counter-elite, professional revolutionaries and *philosophes*, ineffectiveness of the governmental enforcement apparatus, development of an effete ruling class, and elements of duality in power.

For instance, there was no upward mobility except through the Party and Church hierarchy. This caused the alienation of a large group of intellectuals and technocrats. New *philosophes* emerged, and in Poland (contrary to the Anglo-Saxon countries), the intellectuals do enjoy authority.

The intellectuals formed semi-legal opposition organizations such as the KOR, the League for Independent Poland and the ROPCiO. KOR acted as an information bureau and the center for the opposition. The League for Independent Poland conducted political activities and published books without censorship: illegal magazines and papers were plentiful. The Movement for the Defense of Human Rights (MDHR-ROPCiO) stirred up trouble for the regime everywhere.

Professional revolutionaries of the Walesa sort emerged. It must be remembered that Lech Walesa did not just "appear." The first free union chapter was created around the *samizdat* journal, *Robotnik*, in Radom in November, 1977. A "Workers' Committee" was set up in February, 1978 in Katowice; it appealed to workers to form free trade unions. The appeal was signed by Kazimierz Switon, Wladyslaw Sulecki, Tadeusz Kicki, and Roman Kosciuszek (later Solidarity activists). The Committee of Free Trade Unions for the Baltic Coast was formed in May of 1978. Its declaration was signed by Andrzej Gwiazda, Antoni Sokolowski, and Krzysztof Wyszkowski, all names significant in Solidarity. Among others, Lech Walesa was a founding member of that union.

The situation for the revolutionaries was simplified through teachings of Party history and that of the Bolsheviks. These were ready-made models for action and organizational suggestions. For instance, it is ironic that Gomulka was an eminent organizer of sit-in strikes in pre-war Poland, and that those strikes, once employed in the revolutionary history of Poland, were now known as "Polish strikes."

The importance of a core of leading revolutionary activists is well known to even a casual reader of the history of the Bolsheviks. The theories of exploitation were taught in all the high schools. Indeed, in one of the many contradictions of which Marxist dialectics are so fond, the Party, in its pathetic attempt at socialization, sowed the seeds of its own destruction.

When the strike erupted in August, 1980 at Lenin's Shipyard in Gdansk, there were KOR intellectuals on hand who gave tactical—and in this case—moderate advice, as did Bogdan Borusewicz. The activist Walesa climbed over the fence almost at once; and shortly a whole group of intellectual experts, a strange mixture of Catholics and ex-Marxists, arrived.

Even before the strikers won in Gdansk, there was a tentative "duality of power" in Poland. It was in many cases more profitable to be on the opposition's side than on the authorities'. Now the classic "duality of power" appeared, including elements of mob rule and coercion.

Solidarity was effectively in power after signing the "Accord." The next step should have been, logically, a formalization of the de facto situation and an exchange of elites, achieved peacefully or violently. The revolutionary moderate leaders should have been replaced in their turn by the radicals, then the "Thermidorean Reaction" would have set in, and there would have been a normalization of the situation.

But in Poland the revolution did not run its natural course. It was frozen before the climax. In the present global system, practically bipolar, Poland is a part of the Soviet international system. The realization that whatever was going on in Poland was of primary importance and interest to the Soviet Union inhibited the free development. The thought that the Russians might invade Poland was not incredible to any Pole.

The moderate leaders of Solidarity were in a situation similar to their counterparts in the Party. Their freedom of maneuver was also limited by the Soviets. And, at the same time, these leaders were quite aware that they could lose control of the masses or be replaced by their own hot-headed radical colleagues. In this unnatural situation of halting or semi-revolution, their power became destructive and negative. As in the ancient Polish *Sejm* of the elective monarchy, they might put the *liberum veto* (or "free veto") to any motion, while accomplishing very little of a constructive nature.

The Russians too found themselves in an awkward situation. They had lost an opportune moment to intervene in August, 1980, and now the invasion might become a full-scale Russo-Polish war, of which they had already had an unpleasant foretaste, including their defeat in the Polish-Bolshevik War in 1919-1920.

Further, the Russians already had a war going at the other end of their empire, in Afghanistan. In addition, the global climate of opinion had changed: there would be further Soviet disgrace; possible repercussions in the Third World countries; protests of "no longer meek" Communist parties in Western Europe; the anger of the international labor movement; and consequences from the United States and Great Britain, and possibly from other countries; plus the fact that there was now a Polish Pope in the Vatican (though he had no tank divisions to be reckoned with). There would be a further build-up of armaments, which Russia could hardly afford in her present economic situation. Also, the possible conquest of Poland would have involved a costly occupation, with continuing resistance by the underground (plans for which, including caches of arms, conspiratory cells in the Army, and civil disobedience, had already been prepared). Occupied Poland would be an economic burden and a political embarrassment to the Soviet Union.

How could the situation actually develop? It was in the Russian national interest to promote a Finlandization of Poland, but it must be remembered that Russian politics are even less rational than that of most countries, and often difficult to discern.

In Poland (here there is another similarity to other revolutions), the majority of the population, in spite of its anti-Sovietism, was wholeheartedly tired of the tug-of-war between Solidarity and the Government. But the system had obviously misfunctioned and needed to be changed or repaired. The old system might have been reintroduced through a Soviet military intervention and physical elimination of millions of people, although this was not a likely prospect after the events of 1980. Such a change could also have been achieved without a military intervention, by starving Poland—also a risky alternative for Russia, as this course might have led to insurrection.

If all the parties involved had had enough political wisdom, the system could have been repaired by co-opting Solidarity as a junior partner of the Party. If the Solidarity leaders had been given formal responsibility for the fate of their own country, they might have lost some of their revolutionary zeal, and become more aware of the complexities of governing a modern industrialized state. Thus with the problem of recruitment partially solved, and upward mobility introduced, the system would have received a new lease on life.

Politically, Poland obviously had to remain in the Soviet bloc. Her foreign policy would be Moscow-directed, but Soviet intervention in her internal affairs would be minimal. Once some sincerity in Polish-Soviet relations had been introduced, political realism might win out. The Polish people have an immense ability for adaptation, but the impalpable Orwellian model is one of the hardest to digest for human beings brought up in the Western tradition.

An internal political arrangement between the Party and Solidarity would have been reminiscent of the Anglo-Saxon two-party system, but one in which the Communist Party would have been assured its beloved leading role. But both elements would have been responsible to the nation for their errors, through the personal accountability of members for their job performances; and now the legal and loyal opposition party would have been able to articulate the various interests [It is interesting to observe that the Moslems allowed their Christian subject populations the freedom of religion and local autonomy, but the Marxist "religion" wants a government of souls. Communists want to be loved and believed; simple obedience and loyalty is not enough]. And then the government would have been willing and able to perform its conversion function.

As, probably, only one official opposition party would have been permitted—Solidarity—there would have been in its ranks a whole spectrum of political opinion, with numerous factions to allow the political game to continue without danger.

On the other hand, in such a situation it is conceivable that Solidarity as a party would shortly have begun to resemble its communist counterpart. Robert Michels's iron law of oligarchy had already been at work in Solidarity, with evidence of a growing level of bureaucracy, a privileged elite, and attempts at centralizing the workers' councils.

Nevertheless, such an arrangement would certainly have been an improvement, and the reformed two-chambered *Sejm* and semi-independent judiciary would have served as an important regulatory mechanism. With the dismantlement of the state terror apparatus, Solidarity would have been responsible for social discipline. But to achieve that model, greater leaders than the barely literate Lech Walesa or the hot-headed Gwiazda, Rulewski, or Jurczyk, were called for. A man of the caliber of Roman Dmowski was necessary. The men who led Solidarity have shown a total lack of political expertise and arrogance, an unbelievable (for people brought up under Communism) ignorance of Party semantics and psychology. It is hard not to reflect that Walesa was but a man of the moment who became a symbol of forces which he was unable to control.

Solidarity refused the proffered junior partnership with the Party, in spite of the fact that any other realistic alternative was practically impossible, given the present position of the Polish state. The future of Poland was not a rosy one even when Solidarity was at the crossroads; if we imagine a situation in which Poland had been left alone in a kind of international political vacuum, with Solidarity winning a free election, it still would have found itself in a critical position, with no easy solutions. Any government of Poland would have had to apply strong measures, and these measures, of course, must necessarily be unpopular; this is one of the first lessons of applied democracy which the Solidarity leaders would have learned. Perfectly reasonable but unpopular means are not accepted by voters. There are no "quick fixes" to Poland's economic and political problems. The new government would have found itself in the shoes of the former one, *ad infinitum*, until some dictator appeared, just as Jaruzelski actually arrived, though through a shortcut in the above scenario, since he acted quasi-legally within the constitutional framework, martial law being rubberstamped by the docile new *Sejm*.

Let us specuate a moment longer. In a hypothetical situation, the victorious Solidarity might have decided to reintroduce a free economy. No doubt, the capitalistic hand would have mended matters within a few years, but it also would have strangled many in the process: the weak and poor would have cried out, and the Government would have fallen before its cure could ever take effect.

Out of many possible models, the one which combined Finlandization with the PUWP-Solidarity collaboration offered internally and internationally the best chance of success, had Solidarity accepted it as its political goal.

But on December 13, 1981 took place one of the quickest and most successful counterrevolutions in world history, a coup which will undoubtedly become a classic case study for any student of revolutionary phenomena. All speculations about possible development became, at this point, academic. Thousands of Solidarity activists were rounded up and dispatched to detention camps, the entire National Commission and Lech Walesa included. The full paraphernalia of modern military might were displayed, though hardly used. Western broadcasts to Poland were jammed, and foreign correspondents neutralized. The schools and universities were closed.

The Military Council of National Salvation (WRON-Wojskowa Rada Ocalenia Narodowego) headed by General Jaruzelski took over, and martial law was introduced for the first time in a communist state. Attempts at strikes and other forms of resistance were extinguished swiftly and efficiently, almost bloodlessly. The number of victims killed was less than a hundred (i.e., less than those killed in auto crashes during major American holidays, and perhaps less than those shot during any successful communist *coup d'etat* against a capitalistic government).

The denouement came as a surprise not only to Solidarity and the world, but also to seasoned Moscow and Warsaw watchers. But there had been many warning signals. The Party and Jaruzelski had stated repeatedly that any means necessary would be used to prevent fratricidal struggle. The Army's preparedness and loyalty were constantly stressed. The Army paper *Zolnierz Wolnosci* had been more anti-Solidarity than the Party's own paper, *Trybuna Ludu*.

Finally, the ruling elite had found itself in a situation of—almost—no escape. Their options were extremely limited. They had to eliminate the danger to their power—or abdicate. And even if they had, graciously, decided to disappear, under the present political situation, and given Solidarity's hubris, the Brezhnev Doctrine would have added another bloodbath to the many already recorded in Polish history.

Internationally, in a bipolar situation where even a ministate may provoke an atomic holocaust, such a development would be against the will to survive of humankind. Let us also remember that the present unfortunate state of affairs in Eastern Europe is partially the result of the Teheran, Yalta, and Potsdam agreements, and that *realpolitik* should not be mistaken for appeasement.

Jaruzelski's actions were not an invasion by proxy. To the contrary, the deployment of Polish soldiers probably saved the country from the carnage which would have resulted if Russian and Warsaw Pact armies had invaded Poland. The loyalty of the Polish troops was, certainly, the foremost question in the minds of communist rulers. The decision was not lightly nor hastily undertaken, since the current elite has learned the burden and responsibility of power. Certainly, the coup was planned for a long time in advance and with the knowledge and cooperation of the Soviets, but it was executed only after Solidarity rejected the proposal for a government of national accord, and only when the ghost of free elections started to haunt the chambers of Central Committees in Warsaw and Moscow. Solidarity finally overreached itself, and failed utterly, probably bringing down in the process all the freedoms gained during the previous 18 months.

What is to be done? Poland's national interest demands an end to economic anarchy: measures must be taken to raise productivity, reintroduce the civilized conditions of life, and repay the foreign debt. Poland has lived beyond its economic means for more than a decade, and is now paying a high price for its collective national irresponsibility. All the appeals for sabotages, strikes and slowdowns are counterproductive and suicidal, both internally and externally. The time of Solidarity has unfortunately ended.

In its 469 days, Solidarity achieved gains unprecedented in the Eastern bloc. The climate of political opinion was changed. There was absolute freedom of speech and an approximation of the free press. Solidarity put its stamp on Party men, who started to feel and move like real people, not Marxist automata. There was, indeed, a viable chance for *odnowa*.

But it also brought about economic and political chaos, and the clear danger of Soviet occupation. Solidarity went too far too fast; it never had the time to mature politically, to gain seasoned, responsible leaders. Ultimately, it sowed the seeds of its own destruction, and reaped its harvest in full.

Still, Solidarity has altered the Polish political system forever, with repercussions reaching throughout all of Eastern Europe; its impact may yet change the line of political development in the Soviet bloc, and provide hope for the millions of people who presently have none. Solidarity was a great and glorious social experiment cut down in its prime, the massive outpouring of a repressed people. Not just an economic revolution, it provided an outlet for the expression of generations of pent-up emotions, feelings which Jaruzelski and his successors and "fraternal comrades" still must recognize and deal with if the pattern of Polish history holds true. General Jaruzelski has a short period of time—a year, two years, maybe five or ten at most—in which to act and introduce significant reforms, before he too is held accountable for his actions. The drama has not ended, the curtain has not yet fallen—we are merely witnessing the beginning of a new act. The people—and history—will make the final judgment.

Appendices

Appendix A

"On the Present Methods of Prosecution of Illegal Anti-Socialist Activity"

STATEMENT OF THE
Presidium of NSZZ Solidarity,
Mazowsze Region,
Warsaw, November 21, 1981

On November 20, 1980 at 4:30 p.m., security and police functionaries led by Deputy Prosecutor, Mrs. W. Bardonowa, searched the headquarters of the NSZZ Solidarity, Mazowsze region. During the search they confiscated a document on the subject of law and order in our country. That document is entitled: "On the Present Methods of Prosecution of Illegal Anti-Socialist Activity," and it was sent on October 30, 1980 by the Chief Prosecutor, L. Czubinski, to the institutions subordinate to him.

The document reveals many cases of arbitrary police decisions amounting to abuse of power and infringement of the law. Moreover, it takes them totally for granted, proving thereby that the Prosecutor's Office has been used as a tool by the security apparatus. The aim of the document is to show that the emergence of independent trade unions is a direct result of all "anti-socialist" activity. This means that a large section of the judiciary has not accepted the Gdansk agreement. Under the circumstances, it bodes ill that the Chief Prosecutor advises his subordinates to "use skillfully the enclosed text in their political and professional work."

On the day after the search of the union headquarters, Jan Narozniak, a volunteer for union printing work, was summoned to the Ministry of Internal Affairs for questioning, and detained there.

We are warning the authorities not to return to repression. We demand the immediate release of Jan Narozniak. If he is detained any longer, we shall have to call a strike alert in selected enterprises of the Mazowsze region.

At the same time, we demand that L. Czubinski's role in violating the law in the past decade be revealed, especially his responsibility for the persecution of workers at Ursus and Radom after June, 1976.

Statement of Zbigniew Bujak,
Chairman of the Mazowsze region Presidium of
NSZZ Solidarity

I hereby state that although I was not aware of the presence of the text in question on the premises of the Mazowsze Solidarity union or of its duplication, had I known about it I would have ordered it to be duplicated in a number of copies sufficient to distribute to every circle of our union. This text poses a threat to the interests of NSZZ Solidarity.

THE PROSECUTOR'S PLAN FOR A CRACKDOWN

I enclose a document "On the Present Methods of Prosecution of Illegal Anti-Socialist Activity," to be used skillfully in political and professional work.—Lucjan Czubinski, Chief Prosecutor of the Polish People's Republic, Warsaw, October 30, 1980.

The activities of illegal anti-socialist groups, originating among the intelligentsia, began towards the end of the 1950s. They involved chiefly junior academics and students of Warsaw University, with the cooperation of a group of intellectuals in Krakow.

In their initial stage, they took the form of discussion meetings of students and social gatherings, with lectures on subjects of a political and economical nature, followed by debates which presented a distorted picture of the system of the PPR (Polish People's Republic) and other socialist states, detracted from their achievements, and criticized the direction of their further development.

Towards the end of 1964, the Security Service, in the course of a search in the home of a member of the "Warsaw Group," Stanislaw Gomulka, found a document called, "A Program of the Working Class."

Subsequent investigations have shown that it had been written chiefly by Karol Modzelewski and Jacek Kuron, with the cooperation of Stanislaw Gomulka and Bernard Tejkowski.

A few months later, it was revealed that Mr. Modzelewski and Mr. Kuron had written an "Open Letter" to the local group of the PUWP (Polish United Workers' Party) and members of the ZMS (Union of Socialist Youth) at Warsaw University. Both documents, which were clearly hostile to socialism, were largely devoted to an exposition of Trotskyite-revisionist ideas, and, in fact, called for the overthrow of the system of the PPR by force.

It is highly significant that, among a number of revisionist recommendations, the "program" demanded the creation of trade unions that would be independent of the state, giving the working class the right to strike, and replacing the unified party of the working class with several parties competing with each other.

As a result, K. Modzelewski and J. Kuron were arrested, tried, and convicted of an attempt to overthrow the system of the PPR by force.

In separate proceeding, Kazimierz Badowski, Ludwik Has, and Romuald Smiech were arrested, tried, and convicted on a similar charge.

At the same time, a number of persons were persecuted for contacts with centers of ideological diversion abroad, and for supplying them with materials slandering the system and the authorities of the PPR.

In 1968, the following persons, among others, were arrested, tried, and convicted of such charges: Maciej Kozlowski, Maria Tworkowska, Krzysztof Szymborski, Jakub Karpinski, and Maria Szpakowska (the so-called "Taterniks"), all of Warsaw University.

In June and July of 1970, there followed the arrest, trial, and conviction of 30 members of an illegal political organization, "Ruch" (Movement). In this organization were assembled a number of educated people in Lodz, Warsaw, and Lublin who had close connections with the clergy. The leaders were the four brothers Czuma: Hubert, Lukasz, Andrzej, and Benedykt.

Their program was clearly anti-socialist. It favored an unlimited right to private property, denied the role of the working class as the driving force of the nation, and questioned the leading role of the workers' party. The activities of "Ruch" consisted of working out and spreading an ideology hostile to socialism, and later of terrorist acts (an attempt to blow up the statue of Lenin in Poronin).

Apart from these most important activities of anti-socialist groups in the 1960s and 1970s, a number of other cases of hostile anti-socialist actions were exposed. These were also dealt with by means of judicial reprisals (for example, the arrest, trial, and conviction of Melchior Wankowicz, the arrest of Stanislaw Salmonowicz, and others).

In connection with the so-called March events of 1968, and later with the so-called December events of 1970, as well as with the events of 1976 (at Ursus and Radom), similar judicial action was taken against persons guilty of offenses against public order and social property.

The disturbances of 1976 in Radom and Ursus were followed by a considerable activization of anti-socialist forces, which embarked on large-scale action, including actions involving violations of criminal law.

In September, 1976 there came into being an illegal association which called itself the Workers' Defense Committee (KOR), consisting of a number of people who for years engaged in anti-socialist activities (J. Kuron, J. Litynski, A. Maciarewicz, A. Michnik, H. Mikolajska, and others). This association (on September 29, 1977) transformed itself into the Committee of Social Solidarity (KOR), which has since been engaged in activities, some of which have the character of criminal offenses.

The increasing activity of persons who, after the Radom-Ursus events, continued to stimulate social unrest which could result in further violations of public order [for example, there was an attempt to use the Juvenalia celebrations in Krakow as an occasion for disturbances by spreading false rumors on the cases of the death of a student named Pyjas] made it necessary to start an investigation, and to arrest temporarily in May of 1977 the seven persons most actively engaged in criminal activities: Jacek Kuron, Adam Michnik, Antoni Maciarewicz, Piotr Naimski, Wojciech Ostrowski, Jan Jozef Lipski.

These men were suspected of having cooperated with foreign organizations hostile to Poland—Radio Free Europe, Institut Litteraire in Paris,

"Aneks," and others—against the political interests of the Polish People's Republic; and of feeding them specially-concocted false information and papers on the social and political conditions in Poland.

The investigation confirmed these facts, that these men conceived, printed, and distributed information containing false news concerning, among others, reprisals against persons guilty of infringing the law.

Wide distribution of such news could have led to further disturbances of public order. However, investigations failed to supply adequate evidence of the existence of direct links of the people involved with hostile foreign organizations, such as Radio Free Europe and the journal *Kultura* in Paris. Preparatory proceedings against all these people were quashed on the basis of the amnesty decree of July 20, 1977.

The years 1977-1980 saw an increase in the organizational strengthening of anti-socialist elements. Besides KSS-KOR, other organizations came into being, such as the Movement for the Defense of Human and Civil Rights, the Students' Solidarity Committees, the Peasants' Self-Defense Committees, the Movement of Young Poland, and the Confederation for Independent Poland.

These organizations gained ever-wider influence by means of large-scale publishing and propaganda activities. About 30 periodical publications (newspapers, bulletins, magazines) were being edited, printed, and distributed. A number of new brochures were published and several books were printed. A number of titles had a circulation of several thousand copies. Tens of thousands of leaflets were distributed, spreading views and slogans of anti-socialist groups directed against established authority.

These publishing activities were conducted without the approval of the Central Office for the Control of the Press, Publications, and Performances (GUKPPiW), which is an offence against Article 6 of the Decree of August 5, 1946, the law which established the GUKPPiW.

It has been decided that those organizations active in this illegal criminal publishing activity can be treated as offenders against Article 276, p. 1 of the Criminal Code. It is also possible to invoke Article 273, p. 3 of the Criminal Code in qualifying the activities of persons playing a leading part in KSS-KOR and other illegal operations.

Regulations of the criminal law may also be useful in considering the contents of some papers, such as Leszek Moczulski's "Revolution without Revolution," which is, in fact, the program of ROPCiO (the Movement for the Defense of Human and Civil Rights), which aims to seize power (if need be, by force) through anti-socialist elements.

It must be emphasized that the author, in presenting his version of an overthrow of the system in Poland, states that this will be preceded by a period of ever-increasing growth of the political, anti-socialist forces, of expansion of the free press, of local self-government and independent trade unions. In other words, this will be a period during which a power will be forged that can take over the state.

In recent years, methods of dealing with persons engaged in anti-socialist activities have changed. The idea of arranging criminal trials has been abandoned in favor of purely administrative preventive action to preserve order.

The types of actions which were undertaken by the Security Services to limit the negative activities launched by organized anti-socialist groups, and to counter the creation and distribution of illegal publications, as well as to isolate anti-socialist elements from their social and professional environment included the following:

1. Numerous searches of suspected anti-socialist centers which brought to light large quantities of illegally-produced publications destined for mass distribution, as well as equipment for producing and stencilling them.

2. Confiscation and withholding of such items;

3. Detention of persons by the police in order to stop their anti-socialist activities;

4. Applications to tribunals responsible for petty offenses to punish persons who in the course of their anti-socialist activities commit such offenses.

The role of public prosecutors in these actions consisted of:

5. Approving searches and the confiscation of objects seized in the course of searches, as well as issuing orders for the searches to be carried out;

6. In several cases persons engaged in anti-socialist activities were prosecuted for ordinary crimes;

7. Twice—in December, 1979 and in August, 1980—temporary detention for several days was used against groups of persons engaged in anti-socialist activites.

Ad 1: Such searches are, strictly speaking, one of the main ways of counteracting the influence of anti-socialist elements on society which they exert through the illegal manufacture and distribution of propaganda. These raids are carried out by members of the Security Service (SB) and the police (MO), on orders of the officers commanding SB and MO units.

Mostly, these are searches in houses, but also personal searches (for example, of persons detained for distributing something). They are usually carried out in regard to persons engaged in anti-socialist activities. The results are almost always positive; witness the fact that, out of some 200 searches carried out in the second quarter of this year, only a few proved fruitless.

Ad 2: The searches yielded large quantities of various illegal publications, among them periodicals such as *Robotnik (The Worker), Glos, Biuletyn Informacyjny, Krytyka, Dziennik Polski, Zapis, Biuletyn Dolnoslaski Zeszyty Towarzystaw Kursow Naukowych (Bulletins of the Society of Lower Silesia), Zeszyty Historyczne, Zeszyty Towarzystwa Kursow Naukowych (Bulletins of the Society of Scientific Studies), Gazeta Polska, Rzeczpospolita, PPN, Gospodarz, Aneks Postep, Placowka, Bratniak* (Students Organization), *Uczen Polski (Polish School Pupil)*, and *Robotnik Wybrzeza (Sea Coast Worker)*.

The findings included books and brochures published illegally by the so-called Independent Publishing House, Nowa, as well as single publications such as *Revolution Without Revolution, On Trade With the West, Crisis of Breakthrough, The Authorities and the Opposition, Facing the Future, After the Great Leap, In the Middle of Life, Poisoned Humanities, Song of the Rebel, How Long Are We to Suffer, To All Working People, The Story of Katyn, The Black Book of Censorship in the PPR, Notes on the Hungarian Revolution*, and others.

Other confiscated material included large numbers of various leaflets, appeals, and posters calling on the people to protest against various moves of the authorities and to support anti-socialist activities.

Further, a certain amount of unauthorized literature from abroad, particularly publications of the Institut Litteraire in Paris, were found. The number of copies seized varied from search to search, from single items to many hundreds. In the first quarter of this year, a total of some 10,000 copies of various publications have been seized.

The searches also resulted in the confiscation of a certain amount of equipment and materials for the manufacture of illegal publications—typewriters, duplicators, ink, paper, and others.

Ad 3: Detentions were usually effected in connection with various meetings of leading members of anti-socialist organizations, or of the "editorial boards" of illegal publications. Those detained were persons who stencilled, printed, or distributed illegal publications, or who were in possession of such materials. They were detained in local police cells.

Members of the Security Service conducted, or tried to conduct with them, conversations of an explanatory, conscience-forming character, mostly without any result.

As a rule, those detained were usually released within 48 hours. In exceptional cases, such as in August, 1980, the total period of detention of several persons exceeded the legal norm. Several leading activists of anti-socialist groups (Mr. Kuron, Mr. Michnik, and others) were successively held in several police cells for 48 hours each time.

Complaints addressed to the public prosecutor are evidence that these persons were, in fact, freed within 48 hours, but on leaving the police station they were again arrested and held for the next 48 hours. The complaints are proof that between successive detentions the persons were allowed to have a walk, a cup of coffee at a bar, or to buy fruit.

Ad 4: In a number of cases, people engaged in anti-socialist activities were punished by Tribunals for Petty Offenses. These included: illegal assembly (Code of Petty Offenses, Article 51, p. 1), spreading leaflets (dropping litter in public places, Article 145), shouting slogans (Article 51, p. 2), illegal gathering in the streets (Article 50 of the Criminal Code), wearing without permission a badge of the Confederation of Independent Poland (Article 61, p. 1, Code of Petty Offenses).

Data supplied to the Prosecutor-General by the Investigation Bureau of the Ministry of the Interior showed that the total number of persons sentenced in this way in the second quarter of this year was 31. In most cases, the sentence was a fine, in several cases imprisonment. Applications for punishment were issued by the local police station. In cases of appeal from the Tribunal for Petty Offenses to a court, public prosecutors appeared in the appeal trial.

Ad 5: The role of public prosecutors in counteracting defense moves consisted, among others, in carrying out the functions involved in the preparation of a trial. At the moment, the Investigation Bureau and Investigation Departments of Regional Police Commands are in the course of carrying out, under the supervision of public prosecutors, preliminary procedures in 15 cases involving criminal activities of members of anti-socialist groups.

These are under way in the following localities: Warsaw (two cases),

Gdansk, Lublin, Katowice, Cracow, Poznan, Torun, Radom, Szczecin, Wroclaw, Lodz, Rzeszow, Walbrzych, and Kalisz. In such cases the prosecutors usually approved searches carried out by the police, as well as the confiscation of objects found in the course of these searches.

The basis of approval were the results of the searches, in the form of publications issued and distributed by anti-socialist groups. The contents of these publications are usually judged in the light of Articles 271 or 273 of the Criminal Code.

It must be emphasized that in cases where the content of the publication was unimpeachable from the point of view of criminal law, as a basis for approving a search and for confiscation, it was sufficient proof that the publication was the result of the criminal act of its having been printed without the consent of the Central Office for the Control of the Press, Publications, and Performances.

The large number of confiscated objects—typewriters, duplicators, paper, and above all illegal publications—in some cases creates problems of storage. It has therefore been decided, on the basis of Article 201, p. 1 of the Code of Criminal Procedure, *to transfer the publications to the waste paper disposal unit.*

Ad 6: Several persons engaged in anti-socialist activities who had committed common crimes were brought to court for criminal trials. In the second quarter of this year, nine such cases were initiated, and several of them resulted in convictions.

These were crimes committed in connecton with anti-socialist activity, or unconnected with it. In the first group were such offenses as stealing paper, a typewriter, a duplicator, or smuggling a duplicator into the country; in the second, beating or threatening to beat somebody, threatening to use a knife and conspiring to use a knife, and conspiring to obtain a false statement.

Ad 7: In December, 1979, and towards the end of August of this year, preliminary procedures current at the time involved temporary detention in the case of several of the active oppositionists; since, if they had been at large to continue their subversive activities, they might have caused serious public disturbances (in December, 1979, in the Gdansk coastal area, or in August of this year in connection with strikes throughout the country).

In December, 1979, in cases conducted under the supervision of public prosecutors in Warsaw and Lodz, 15 persons were detained. In August, 1980, 21 persons were detained in Warsaw, and seven in other cities—a total of 28 persons. They were arrested under Article 276 of the Criminal Code, that is, for crimes committed by virtue of being members of associations (KSS-KOR, ROPCiO) pursuing the criminal activity of producing and distributing various publications without permission from the GUKPPiW.

The basic evidence which justified the detentions of August, 1980 consisted in the first place of large numbers of illegal socio-political and economic publications, seized in the course of searches carried out in the suspects' homes.

Information contained in these publications was designed to cause social unrest, it was tendentious, full of demagoguery, sometimes quite false, although not always falling under the specifications of Articles 270,

271, or 273 of the Criminal Code. In all cases, however, it was published without the consent of the Central Office for the Control of the Press, Publications, and Performances, and thus qualified as a crime under Article 6A of the Decree of August 5, 1946.

The character, quantity, and contents of these publications, as well as the methods of their production and distribution, were unequivocal evidence of an organized publishing activity carried out in the framework of the above-mentioned illegal political organizations.

Some of these publications even stated quite openly that they were issued by these organizations. Some articles were signed by persons who thereby admitted, as it were, their activities within these illegal organizations. The extent of the publication activities thus exposed and documented indicated that this, indeed, was one of the most important purposes of these organizations at the present stage.

All of these facts were taken into consideration when detentions were ordered, as well as in the formulation of charges concerning the involvement of these persons in associations (illegal political organizations) formed for the purpose of committing a crime (publishing without the consent of the Central Office for the Control of the Press, Publications, and Performances).

It must be said, however, that the evidence on which the detention orders were based was not sufficient, and, if the investigations were to be completed, the indictments would have to be considerably enriched.

This will necessitate in the first place the acquisition of some personal evidence (explanations given by the suspects, depositions of witnesses) which would make it possible to assemble adequate proof of the guilt of the arrested persons. In view of the fact that persons involved in anti-socialist activities have in recent years adopted the tactics of refusing, as a rule, to make any statements in the course of the preparatory procedure, the task of acquiring such personal evidence encounters considerable difficulties.

It is absolutely necessary to pay much more attention to the problem of documenting much more extensively than in the past the effects of the criminal activities of anti-socialist groups.

At present, deeds of those persons taking part in anti-socialist activities are treated as participation in an association whose purpose is to produce and distribute illegal publications (offenses under Article 276 of the Criminal Code). However, some actions of these groups go beyond the specifications of this law.

From some articles and public statements of members of anti-socialist groups, it is clear that they also envision the possibility, even the need to take over power in the state, by force if necessary. Nowadays, they declare this quite openly.

Preparations for the implementation of such ideas could serve as grounds for qualifying this activity, from the point of view of criminal law, as action preparatory to, or even initiating, the overthrow of the system established in Poland. Therefore, in securing more extensive evidence, an account should be taken of the need of selecting and recording evidence that would permit also the formulation of such charges. General Public Prosecutor's Office, Departments II and III, Warsaw, October, 1980. [Oliver MacDonald, ed., *The Polish August* (San Francisco: Ztangi Press, 1981), pp. 145-155. It is worth noting that, for all his troubles, Lucjan Czubinski was ultimately sacrificed to Solidarity—i.e., dismissed.]

Appendix B

An Open Letter to Shipyard Workers
and All Coastal Workers,
by Jacek Kuron

I am turning to you because it is mainly due to you that I and my colleagues in the Social Self-Defense Committee "KOR" were released from prison on September 1st. Our release was one of the demands of the Gdansk Agreement. I am writing to you because today the whole propaganda machinery of the Polish People's Republic is turned against me and "KOR" with the aim of destroying your achievement: trade unions. the authorities were forced to agree to independent and self-governing trade unions, but there are still some who hope they will be able to deprive the trade unions of this independence. The unions are strong thanks to your courage and solidarity, thanks to the genuine activists chosen, controlled, and supported by you. The campaign of slander is directed against your courage, and its instigators want you to abandon your leaders one by one. On the surface, it concerns Kuron, but soon it may concern Anna Walentynowicz, Lech Walesa, Andrzej Gwiazda, Anna Duda-Gwiazda, Andrzej Kolodziej, Alina Pienkowska, and Jacek Pilichoski, who—as the statement of the *Solidarnosc* Coordination Committee of September 24, 1980 points out—were defended by the "KOR" when dismissed from work, and imprisoned for their struggle for independent trade unions. At first sight the matter only concerns Kuron, but in fact the authorities want you to accept that they can decide who has and has not the right to be active in trade unions. And then they will choose union leaders acceptable to themselves. There are still people who believe that they can imitate Goebbels: to lie and lie again until the lies stick.

I have the honor to be a member of the "KOR" which, from the 1st of July, i.e., when the strikes began, has appealed to workers to organize themselves peacefully, and has appealed to the authorities not to cause a national tragedy, but to talk with the democratically-elected workers' representatives. Polish television maintains that in an interview given to the Swedish television I incited workers to set fire to party committees. In fact, in July and August, warning the authorities against using force against the strikers, I reminded them of the party committees set on fire in December, 1970 and June, 1976. At that time I repeated: "Do not burn down party committees—set up your own instead." It is strange that Polish television should make me responsible for the blood of coastal workers. But miracles of television technology will not help them put the blame for the December, 1970 massacre and 1976 tortures on me or on "KOR." We all know now that we—workers, intellectuals, farmers—are responsible for our country, not party secretaries and ministers. And you, the workers at the Coast, and the Silesian miners who support you, the Ursus metal workers, the writers and scholars of Warsaw—demanded the rights and institutions which would enable Poland to develop in peace and freedom. Those who make an outcry about the amount of money your strike has cost have themselves squandered billions of dollars in foreign credits. It is they who are responsible for the present situation, and for the lack of opportunity for any real improvements within the next few years. We have to face them calmly, even if they should again try to provoke unrest.

On September 23, 1976 we formed the Workers' Defense Committee with over a dozen people. We were ashamed that the intelligentsia had been silent in 1970 and '71, and we wanted to restore its good name. After the brutal suppression of workers' strikes and demonstrations, thousands of workers all over Poland found themselves without jobs. Police jails were full. Trials began in Warsaw (Ursus) and Radom. Thousands of workers were brutally beaten and tortured. "KOR" set for itself the aim of organizing financial help for people dismissed from work and for the families of the imprisoned, to offer legal and—when necessary—medical help, to fight for freedom for the imprisoned and jobs for those sacked. The Workers' Defense Committee appealed to all Poles here and abroad for moral and financial support, and therefore from the very start received large sums of money, since people both at home and abroad responded generously to the appeal.

The emergence of "KOR" activated wide sections of the nation. About a thousand families persecuted in 1976 received help. To support this, hard work was needed from hundreds of people collecting information about repression, means to help the persecuted, etc. In the course of collecting signatures in defense of the imprisoned, thousands of people were not afraid to sign. Among them were both scientist and artists, teachers and representatives of other professions, as well as workers and farmers. Security forces have not been able to contain the growing social movement, despite beatings, sometimes severe, despite arrests and sackings, threats and slanders.

After the murder by "persons unknown" of the "KOR" collaborator in Krakow, the student Stanislaw Pyjas, and protest demonstrations in Krakow, eleven members and collaborators of "KOR" were arrested. A mass protest action led not only to their release, but also to the release of workers previously sentenced to up to nine years' imprisonment. From that time on, the opposition movement has been spreading: student solidarity committees and farmers' self-defense committees emerged as well as founding committees of free trade unions. In the coastal region the founders included: Lech Walesa, Anna Kolodziej,

Anna Duda-Gwiazda, Bogdan Borusewicz, and other later leaders of the August, 1980 strikes. Many opposition groups and periodicals have emerged, among them *Robotnik* (*The Worker*), well-known to workers throughout Poland (about one million copies reached their readers), edited collectively by intellectuals and workers; *Placowka* (*Outpost*), for farmers and others. In September, 1977, "KOR" was transformed into the Social Self-Defense Committee "KOR," widening the scope of its activities to stand up in defense of all people persecuted for voicing their opinions and for acting in defense of law and order, democracy, freedom of speech and association in civic, religious, political, or professional interests. "KOR" supports independent social initiatives and exposes lawlessness (e.g., murders of persons in police custody were unmasked in *The Book of Lawlessness*).

Since the first strikes in July, 1980, we have gathered and published information about the strikes and workers' demands. We realized that the authorities can only use repression and suppress a strike when nobody knows about it. We knew that one plant's experiences can be of help to others. When on August 18, 1980 the region of the striking Baltic Coast was cut off from the rest of the country, we spread information about the strike, about the formation of the Inter-Factory Strike Committee and its 21 demands to dozens of big enterprises.

On August 20, 1980 over a dozen of more active "KOR" members and collaborators were arrested. This was not my first time in prison, on this occasion for a few days only; but altogether I have spent six years in prison. Now every additional day behind bars is more difficult. It is obvious that I have very personal reasons for gratitude, and I am turning to you now, when I am being slandered by every possible means in the press, radio, and television. I am approaching the age of 50. I have no position, no property, no titles; my only possession is my good name, of which they are trying to deprive me. They resort to lies, forgery, and provocation, and they have at their disposal the most sophisticated technical means, powerful propaganda machinery, and large sums of money for bribes. You remember well that when the Inter-Factory Strike Committee was formed, it was said that it was the work of anti-socialist elements who had found their way into the ranks of the strikers; in inner circles it was said that "KOR" was directing the Coastal strike action.

I do not know why the West German weekly *Der Spiegel* chose to publish this version of events. But I do know why the Polish press and television repeated it. Some were meant to believe that it was an anti-socialist plot, others to be angry with me for talking such nonsense. The authorities were also hoping that Lech Walesa—called a front-line lieutenant—would take offense. Ridiculous, small-minded people. They do not realize that they only are interested in becoming at any cost generals, secretaries, and ministers. We—Lech, Anna, Andrzej, Bogdan, myself—we are all front-line officers. We are and always want to be in the first line of the struggle for human rights, workers' rights, national rights. As a matter of fact, they have somewhat promoted us, for an officer in the army gives orders, while we can only and want only to listen to the people who are fighting together with us and for whom we are fighting, who believe us and who must control us.

There are many difficult tasks in front of us. Independent and self-governing trade unions will not by themselves bring about more meat in the shops, shorter queues, better transport, more housing. These and all the other goods we need must be produced by a well-organized industry, agriculture, building trade. After many years of hard work, we have learned that its fruits have been wasted, the situation is bad, and will become worse. We cannot count on a good party secretary; we have to organize ourselves democratically and take the affairs of the country into our own hands. Yet full independence is impossible: we have to take into consideration the external forces guarding the leading role of the party in the state. We must consciously give up a part of our independence and concentrate on trade unions which will truly defend workers' rights, on self-government in industry, on farmers' organizations, and on a genuine cooperative movement, on independent student movements, and on independence of research, culture, and education. This is the meaning of the Gdansk agreement, which is mainly your achievement. To fulfill this agreement, not to waste this great national opportunity, is our common task, the task of all Polish citizens who do not think only of personal or group interests. [Oliver MacDonald, ed., *The Polish August* (San Francisco: Ztangi Press, 1981), pp. 142-145.]

Appendix C

The Gdansk Accord

[This protocol was signed on behalf of the strikers by Lech Walesa (President of the MKS), Andrzej Kolodziej and Bogdan Lis (Vice-Presidents), L. Badkowski, W. Gruszewski, A. Gwiazda, S. Izdebski, J. Kwiecik, Z. Kobylinski, H. Krzywonos, S. Lewandowski, A. Pienkowska, J. Przybylski, J. Sikorski, L. Sobieszek, T. Stanny, A. Walentynowicz, and F. Wisniewski. It was signed for the Governmental Commission by: President Mieczyslaw Jagielski (Vice Prime Minister), Z. Zielinski, member of the Secretariat of the Central Committee of the PUWP, T. Fiszbach, President of Gdansk Voievodship, and the Voievod (or mayor) of Gdansk, J. Kolodziejski.]

The governmental commission and the inter-factory Strike Committee (MKS), after studying the 21 demands of the striking workers of the coast, have reached the following conclusions:

—On Point No. 1, which reads: "To accept trade unions as free and independent of the party, as laid down in Convention No. 87 of the ILO and ratified by Poland, which refers to the matter of trade union rights," the following decision has been reached:

1. Trade unions in the Polish People's Republic have not lived up to the hopes and aspirations of the workers. We thus consider it beneficial to create new union organizations, as authentic expressions of the working class. Workers will continue to have the right to join the old trade unions, and we are looking at the possibility of the two union structures cooperating.

2. The MKS declares that it will respect the principles laid down in the Polish Constitution when setting up the new independent and self-governing unions. These new unions are intended to defend the social and material interests of the workers, and not to play the role of a political party. They will be established on the basis of the socialization of the

means of production and of the socialist system which exists in Poland today. They will recognize the leading role of the PUWP in the state, and will not oppose the existing system of international alliances. Their aim is to ensure for the workers the necessary means for the determination, expression, and defense of their interests. The governmental commission will guarantee full respect for the independence and self-governing character of the new unions in their organizational structures and their functioning at all levels. The government will ensure that the new unions have every possibility of carrying out their function of defending the interests of the workers and of seeking the satisfaction of their material, social, and cultural needs. Equally, it will guarantee that the new union will not be the object of any discrimination.

3. The creation and the functioning of free and self-governing trade unions is in line with Convention 87 of the ILO relating to trade union rights, and Convention 97, relating to the rights of free association and collective negotiation, both of which conventions have been ratified by Poland. The coming into being of more than one trade union organization requires changes in the law. The government, therefore, will initiate the necessary legal changes, especially as regards trade unions, workers' councils, and the labor code.

4. The strike committees must be able to turn themselves into institutions representing the workers at the lowest level, whether in the fashion of workers' councils or as preparatory committees of the new trade unions. As a preparatory committee, the MKS is free to adopt the form of a trade union, or of an association of the coastal region. The preparatory committees will remain in existence until the new trade unions are able to organize proper elections. The government undertakes to create the conditions necessary for the recognition of unions outside of the existing Central Council of Trade Unions.

5. The new trade unions should be able to participate in decisions affecting the conditions of workers in such matters as the division of the national assets, the division of social assistance funds (health, education, culture), establishment of wages, including automatic increases of wages in line with inflation, master economic plans, national investment, and prices. The government undertakes to ensure the conditions necessary for the carrying out of these functions.

6. The enterprise committee will set up a research center whose aim will be to engage in an objective analysis of the situation of workers and employees, and will attempt to determine the correct ways in which their interests can be represented. This center will also provide the information and expertise necessary for dealing with such questions as a price index and wage index, and the proper forms of compensation required to deal with price increases. The new unions should have their own publications.

7. The government will guarantee respect for Article I, paragraph 1 of the trade union law of 1949, which guarantees the workers the right freely to come together to form trade unions. The new trade union will not join the Central Council of Trade Unions (CRZZ). It is agreed that the new trade union law will respect these principles. The participation of members of the MKS and of the preparatory committees for the new trade unions in the elaboration of the new legislation is also guaranteed.

THE RIGHT TO STRIKE

—On Point No. 2, which reads: "To guarantee the right to strike, and the security of strikers and those who help them," it has been agreed that:

The right to strike will be guaranteed by the new trade union law. The law will define the circumstances under which strikes can be called and organized, the ways in which conflicts can be resolved, and penalties for infringements of the law. Articles 52, 64 and 65 of the labor code (which outlaw strikes) will cease to have effect from now until the new law comes into practice. The government undertakes to protect the personal safety of strikers and those who have helped them, and to insure against any deterioration in their conditions of work.

FREEDOM OF EXPRESSION

—With regard to Point No. 3, which reads: "To respect freedom of expression and publication, as upheld by the Constitution of the Polish People's Republic, and to take no measures against independent publications, as well as to grant access to the mass media to representatives of all religions," it has been agreed that the following will be added:

1. The government will bring before the *Sejm* within three months a proposal for a law on control of the press, of publications, and of other public media, which will be based on the following principles: censorship must protect the interests of the state. This means the protection of state secrets, and of economic secrets as these will be defined in the new legislation, the protection of state and international interests, the protection of religious convictions, as well as the rights of non-believers, the suppression of publications which offend against morality.

The proposals will include the right to make a complaint against press control to a supreme administrative tribunal. This law will be incorporated as an amendment to the administrative code.

2. Access to the mass media by religious organizations in the course of their religious activities will be provided through an agreement between the state institutions and the religious associations on matters of content and of organization. The government will ensure the transmission by radio of Sunday mass through a specific agreement with the Catholic Church.

3. Radio and television as well as the press and publishing houses must express differing points of view. They must also be under the control of society.

4. The press as well as citizens and their organizations must have access to public documents, and above all to administrative instructions and socio-economic plans, in the form in which they are published by the government and by the administrative bodies which draw them up. Exceptions to the principle of open administration will be legally defined in agreement with Point No. 3, paragraph 1.

—With regard to Point No. 4, which reads: "To reestablish the rights of people who were fired after the strikes in 1970 and 1976, and of students who have been excluded from institutions of higher education because of their opinions; (b) to free all political prisoners, including Edmund

Zadrozynski, Jan Kozlowski, and Marek Kozlowski; (c) to cease repression against people for their opinions," it has been agreed:

(a) to immediately investigate the reasons given for the firings after the strikes of 1970 and 1976. In every case where injustice is revealed, the person involved must be reinstated, taking into account any new qualifications that person may have acquired. The same principle will be applied in the case of students.

(b) The cases of persons mentioned under point (b) should be put to the Ministry of Justice, which within two weeks will study their dossiers. In cases where those mentioned are already imprisoned, they must be released pending this investigation, until a new decision on their case is reached.

(c) to launch an immediate investigation into the reasons for the arrests of those mentioned.

(d) to institute full freedom of expression in public and professional life.

—On Point No. 5, which reads: "To inform the public about the creation of the MKS and its demands, through the mass media," it has been decided that:

This demand shall be met through the publication in all the national mass media of the full text of this agreement.

—On Point No. 6, which reads: "To implement the measures necessary for resolving the crisis, starting with the publication of all the relevant information on the socio-economic situation, and to allow all groups to participate in a discussion on a program of economic reforms, the following has been agreed:

We consider it essential to speed up economic reform. The authorities will work out and publish the basic principles of such reform in the next few months. It is necessary to allow for wide participation in a public discussion of the problem. In particular, the trade unions must take part in the working out of laws relating to state enterprises and to workers' self-management. Economic reform must be based on strengthening autonomous operations, and participation of the workers' councils in management. Specific regulations will be drawn up in order to guarantee that the trade unions will be able to carry out their functions as set out in Point No. 1 of this agreement.

Only a society which has a firm grasp on reality can take the initiative in reforming the economy. The government will significantly increase the areas of socio-economic information to which society, the trade unions, and other social and economic organizations have access.

The MKS also suggests, in order that a proper perspective be provided for the development of the family agricultural units which are the basis of Polish agriculture, that individual and collective sectors of agriculture should have equal access to the means of production, including the land itself, and that conditions should be created for the reestablishment of self-governing co-operatives.

—On Point No. 7, which reads: "To pay all the workers who have taken part in the strike for the period of the strike as if they were on paid holiday throughout this period, with payment to be made from the funds of the CRZZ, the following decision has been reached:

Workers and employees participating in the strike will receive, on their return to work, 40% of their wages. The rest, which will add up to a full

100% of the normal basic wage, will be calculated as would holiday pay, on the basis of an 8-hour working day. The MKS calls on workers who are members to work towards an increase in output, to improve the use of raw materials and energy, and to show greater work discipline, when the strike is over, and to do this in cooperation with the management of factories and state enterprises.

—On Point No. 8, which reads: "To increase the minimum wage for every worker by 2000 zlotys a month to compensate for the increase in prices, the following has been decided:

These wage increases will be introduced gradually, and will apply to all types of workers and employees and in particular to those who receive the lowest wages. The increases will be worked out through agreements in individual factories and branches. The implementation of the increases will take into account the specific character of particular professions and sectors. The intention will be to increase wages through revision of pay scales or through increasing other side benefits.

White collar workers will receive salary increases on an individual basis. These increases will be put into effect between now and the end of September, 1980, on the basis of agreements reached in each branch.

After reviewing the situation in all the branches, the government will present, by October 31, 1980, in agreement with the trade unions, a program of pay increases to come into effect beginning January 1, 1981, starting with those who get the least salary, paying particular attention to larger families.

—On Point No. 9, which reads: "To guarantee a sliding wage scale," the following decision has been reached:

It is necessary to slow down the rate of inflation through stricter control over both the public and private sectors, and in particular through the suppression of hidden price increases.

Investigations will be carried out concerning the cost of living. These studies will be made both by trade unions and by scientific institutions. By the end of 1980, the government will set out the principles of a system of compensation for inflation, and these principles will be open to discussion by the public. When they have been accepted, they will come into effect. It will be necessary to deal with the question of a social minimum in elaborating these principles.

—On Point No. 10, which reads: "To insure the supply of products on the internal Polish market, and to export only surplus goods, and Point No. 11, which reads: "To suppress commercial prices and to ban the use of foreign currency in sales on the internal market," and Point No. 12, which reads: "To introduce ration cards for meat and meat-based products, until the market situation can be brought under control," the following agreement has been reached:

The supply of meat will be increased between now and December 31, 1980, through an increase in the profitability of agricultural production and a limitation on the exports of meat to what is absolutely indispensable, as well as through the import of extra meat supplies. At the same time, during this period a program for the improvement of the meat supply will be drawn up, which will take into account the possibility of the introduction of a rationing system through the issue of cards.

Products which are scarce on the national market for current consumption will not be sold in "Pewex" shops; and between now and the end of the year, the population will be informed of all decisions which are taken concerning the problems of supply.

The MKS has called for the abolition of the special shops and the levelling out of the price of meat and related products.

—On Point No. 13, which reads: "To introduce the principle of cadre selection on the basis of qualifications and not on the basis of membership in the party, and to abolish the privileges of the police (MO) and the security services (SB), and of the party apparatus, through the abolition of special sources of supply, through the equalization of family allowances, etc." we have reached the following agreement:

The demand for cadres to be selected on the basis of qualifications and ability has been accepted. Cadres can be members of the PUWP, of the SD (the Democratic Party, which draws its membership from small private enterprises), of the ZSL (the Peasant Party—these three parties make up the National Front), or of no party. A program for the equalization of family allowances of all the professional groups will be presented by the government before December 31, 1980. The govermental commission states that only employees' restaurants and canteens, such as those in other work establishments and offices, will be operated.

—On Point No. 14, which reads: "To allow workers to retire at 50 years for women and 55 for men, or after 30 years of work for women, and 35 years for men, regardless of age," it has been agreed that:

It is impossible, but the governmental commission declares pensions will be increased each year taking into account the real economic situation and the increase in the lowest wages. Between now and December 1, 1981, the government will work out and present a program on these questions. The government will work out plans for the increase of old age and other pensions up to a social minimum established through studies carried out by scientific institutions; these will be presented to the public and put under the control of the trade unions.

The MKS stresses the great urgency of these matters and will continue to raise the issue until some mechanism is instituted to increase old age and other pensions to account for the high cost of living.

—On Point No. 15, which reads: "To increase the old style pensions to the level paid under the new system," it has been agreed:

The governmental commission states that the lowest pensions will be increased every year as the lowest wages increase. The government will present a program to this effect between now and December 1, 1981. The government will draft proposals for a rise in the lowest pensions to the level of the social minimum as defined in studies made by scientific institutes. These proposals will be presented to the public and subject to control by the unions.

—On Point No. 16, which reads: "To improve working conditions and the health services so as to insure better medical protection for the workers," it has been agreed that:

It is necessary to increase immediately the resources put into the sphere of the health services, to improve medical supplies through the import of basic materials where these are lacking, to increase the salaries of all health workers, and, with the utmost urgency on the part of the government and the ministries, to prepare programs for improving the general health of the population. Other measures to be taken in this area are put forward in the appendix.

—On Point No. 17 which reads: "To insure day care centers for the children of all working women," it has been agreed that: The governmental commission is fully in agreement with this demand. The provincial authorities will present proposals on this question before November 30, 1980.

—On Point No. 18, which reads: "To increase the length of maternity leave to three years to allow a mother to bring up her child," it has been decided that:

Before December 31, 1981, an analysis of the possibilities open to the national economy will be made in consultation with the trade unions, on the basis of which an increase in the monthly allowance for women who are on unpaid maternity leave will be worked out.

The MKS asks that this analysis should include an allowance which will provide 100% of pay for the first year after birth, and 50% for the second year, with a fixed minimum of 2,000 zlotys a month. This goal should be gradually reached from the first half of 1981 onwards.

—On Point No. 19, which reads: "To reduce the waiting period for the allocation of housing," the following agreement has been reached:

The district authorities will present a program of measures for improving the housing situation and for reducing the waiting list for housing, before December 31, 1980. These proposals will be put forward for a wide-ranging discussion in the district, and competent organizations, such as the Polish Town-Planners Association, the Central Association of Technicians, etc., will be consulted. The proposals will be put forward for ways of using present building enterprises and prefabricated housing factories, and to a thoroughgoing development of the industry's production base. Similar action will be taken throughout the country.

—On Point No. 20, which reads: "To increase the travelling allowance from 40 to 100 zlotys, and to introduce a cost-of-living bonus," it has been agreed that:

An agreement will be reached on the question of raising the travelling allowance and compensation, to take effect, from January 1, 1981. The proposals for this to be ready by October 31, 1980.

—On Point No. 21, which reads: "To make Saturday a holiday. In factories where there is continuous production, where there is a four-shift system, Saturday working must be compensated for by a commensurate increase in the number of holidays, or through the establishment of another free day in the week," it has been agreed that:

The principle that Saturday should be a free day should be put into effect, or another method of providing free time should be devised. This should be worked out by December 31, 1980. The measures should include an increase in the number of free Saturdays from the start of 1981. Other possibilities relating to this point are mentioned in the appendix, or appear in the submissions of the MKS.

After reaching the above agreements, it has also been decided that:
The Government undertakes:

—to insure personal security and to allow both those who have taken part in the strike and those who have supported it to return to their previous work under the previous conditions;

—to take up at the ministerial level the specific demands raised by the workers of all the enterprises represented in the MKS;

—to immediately publish the complete text of this agreement in the press, the radio, television, and in the national mass media.

The strike committee undertakes to propose ending the strike from 5:00 p.m. on August 31, 1980.

Protokoly Porozumien Gdansk, Szczecin, Jastrzebie.

K.A.W. "Ruch", Warsaw, 1981

Appendix D

The Constitution of the Independent, Self-Governing Trade Union Solidarity (excerpts)

CHAPTER I. NAME, AREA OF OPERATIONS, HEADQUARTERS
Paragraph 1
The workers have organized a union to be called "The Solidarity Independent, Self-Governing Trade Union," referred to hereinafter as the Union. In accordance with the principles contained in the Constitution of the Polish People's Republic, with those in Conventions Nos. 87 and 98 of the International Labor Organization as ratified by Poland, and in Part I, Points 1-7 of the understanding negotiated by the Interfactory Strike Committee with the Government Commission in Gdansk, the union will seek to protect workers' rights, including their material, social, and cultural rights.

Paragraph 2
The union will operate in the territory of the Polish People's Republic.

Paragraph 3
The headquarters of the union's National Commission is in Gdansk.

CHAPTER II. GENERAL RESOLUTION
Paragraph 4
The union is independent of the administrative organs of the Polish state and its political organizations.

Paragraph 5
The union organizes workers employed on the basis of work contracts (including collective work contracts), and in agricultural cooperatives, on the basis of membership in the cooperative, as well as students in factory-run vocation schools or those receiving vocational training, persons employed in cottage industry, persons performing work on the basis of an agent's agreement (concessions). Loss of work will not result in loss of membership. Retired persons can also be members.

Paragraph 6
The purposes of the union are to protect the rights, dignity, and interests

of workers; and particularly to:

1. Protect the material, social, and cultural interests of its members and their families;

2. Protect the rights of the workers in the performance of their professional work, their remuneration, their social and living conditions, as well as protecting their health and safety at work;

3. Make efforts to harmonize the regular operations of the factory with the interests of the workers;

4. Strengthen the family, as well as family life;

5. Spread democracy and to strengthen collegial solidarity in mutual relations;

6. Provide the workers with opportunities to improve their vocational qualifications;

7. Influence the preparation of economic and social policies;

8. Create an active concern to work for the good of the fatherland.

Paragraph 7

The union will achieve its goals by:

1. Representing its members before employers, authorities, and state administrative agencies, as well as social organizations and institutions;

2. Negotiating and announcing collective work contracts;

3. Providing legal assistance and intervening in cases of conflict between employee and employer;

4. Organizing and directing steps to be taken by personnel protesting cases of actual infringements of the interests of workers; and, in particularly flagrant cases, to call a strike;

5. Devising mutual aid for union members;

6. Undertaking efforts to obtain guaranteed vacations for workers and their families, satisfying their housing needs, obtaining places in day care centers and nursery schools for their children, as well as guaranteeing their proper share of services from their factory social organization;

7. Combating alcoholism;

8. Supporting efforts to improve the economy, to develop culture, education, science, and technical progress;

9. Directing educational-cultural activities, creating opportunities for relaxation after work;

10. Cooperation with the authorities and state administrative agencies in the sphere of work regulations;

11. Maintaining control over observation of safety and health regulations at work, ensuring periodic checkups of work sites, prohibiting its members from working in places not conforming to agreed-upon conditions;

12. Cooperating with the Health Service in protecting the health of workers and their families;

13. Conducting research into the conditions of life of the working masses, particularly on their costs of living;

14. Development of press and publishing efforts;

15. Passing public judgment on projects and regulations affecting the life of working people, workers' representatives, workers' participation in management, social legislation, as well as key decisions on: division of the national income; investment trends; division of the social consumption fund; keeping the market supplied; housing policy; the formation of

prices and pay scales, as well as other essential questions affecting working people.

Paragraph 8

I. The union members are organized on a territorial-vocational basis, which means that:

1. The union organizes members of every trade;

2. The basic union organization is the factory local, organizing workers of every trade employed in a given factory;

3. The factory local will organize, as necessary, lower level units: the employees of small factories can create interfactory union organizations to which employees of factories without union locals can belong;

4. Within the union, professional or branch sections can operate on all levels; professional sections include workers performing one trade or a number of related trades;

II. The union can reach agreements to cooperate with labor unions representing workers of one profession or several related trades if the statutes and operations of those unions correspond to the basic principles contained in the union's statutes.

Paragraph 9

Posts at every level of the union are elective. Elections to such posts are based on the following principles:

1. There are no restrictions on the number of candidates;

2. The vote is for individual candidates;

3. The voting is secret;

4. The chairman—with the exception of the chairman of the National Commission—is directly elected by a general assembly of the organization at the given level;

5. A person can hold one office in the union only for two successive terms;

6. Union office cannot be held by persons occupying executive positions in places of work (directors, deputy directors, supervisors, deputy supervisors of a factory, or directors of divisions in a large enterprise, as well as persons in administrative positions directly subordinate to the management), or fulfilling managerial functions in political organizations;

7. The recall of a union official from office is handled according to the same principles as those governing his election.

Paragraph 10

A union local is formed on the initiative of workers, who create for this purpose a constituent committee. The creation of a union local should be reported to the regional union authorities.

CHAPTER VI. STRIKES

Paragraph 32

After exhausting all other forms of approach, the union can call a strike.

Paragraph 33

1. The strike may be a warning strike or an actual strike.

a. Where the circumstances permit, a real strike should be preceded by a warning strike;

b. A warning strike should not last longer than half a working day;

c. An actual strike lasts until the appropriate union officials announce its conclusion. The ending of a strike may be the subject of an agreement with the employer or with the state authorities.

2. If the cause of the strike is a disagreement in one factory, the strike can be called only after an absolute majority of members of the factory union local vote for it.

3. In cases where the cause of the strike is other than specified in Subparagraph 2, the decision to call a strike is taken by the board of the regional union organization, which at the same time announces the extent of the strike.

4. A resort to repressive measures against union officials and preventing them in this way from carrying out the appropriate decision empowers the employees of the factories to strike immediately.

5. In case the proclamation of a strike in one factory does not produce results, union officials are empowered to call a solidarity strike.

Paragraph 34

The above resolutions do not apply to workers in factories which, because of their nature, cannot strike. In order to support their demands, a solidarity strike can be called.

CHAPTER VII. THE SOCIAL-PROFESSIONAL WORK CENTER AND PUBLICATIONS

Paragraph 40

1. General assemblies of delegates on the regional level decide on how to divide up the monies obtained from membership dues among factory (interfactory, and regional) union organizations.

2. At the same time, the general assembly sets the rules governing social services (allowances, aid).

3. Regional union organizations help finance the operations of all union officials on the basis of directives issued by the union.

CHAPTER IX. INTERIM AND FINAL DECISIONS

Paragraph 43

All matters not covered by the statutes as well as all controversial decisions will be taken up by the National Commission.

K.A.W. "Ruch," Warsaw, 1981

Appendix E

Government's Report on the Economy and a Program of Reform, August, 1981

The State of the Economy

Causes of the crisis related to economic policy:

The "strategy of dynamic development" of the 1970s, which consisted of forcible investment based largely on foreign credit, ended in failure. The economy did not develop harmoniously, which resulted in its growing dependence on imported materials and parts. An uncontrolled boom in demand for goods compounded the inflationary processes and disorganized the market. The economy grew too rapidly.

Causes of the crisis related to mismanagement of the economy:

Many decisions of strategic importance were taken without consultation and were based on faulty information. Expert assessments were frequently false. Many decision makers on all levels lacked appropriate competence. Managers of the economy yielded to pressures from powerful groups controlling different segments of the economy. Economic decisions were forced when the government was presented with *faits accomplis*, such as the illegal launching of investment ventures. As the quality of planning worsened, economic accounts were falsified to make conditions seem better than they were.

General diagnosis of the situation:

The permissible amount of foreign debt has been exceeded. Export capacities are insufficient to provide for a timely repayment of the debt and new financing of new indispensable imports. Too many investment ventures have been launched; some of these businesses cannot now be operated due to a lack of materials and spare parts. The fundamental problem is lack of energy needed by other parts of the economy. Society's purchasing power far exceeds the supply of goods and services desired by the people, and is compounded by worsening inflation and a faulty structure of retail prices, which consolidates a lack of market equilibrium.

Credited imports from the West have steadily increased faster than exports. Over a period of ten years, credits worth 42 billion dollars were used. These included credits for investment goods, grain, and other materials amounting to some 27000 million dollars. By the end of April, Poland owed some 24000 million dollars to its creditors. Because of this burden of debt coming due, new credits have to be obtained to finance imports of goods.

Trade exchanges with socialist countries have a stabilizing influence on the Polish economy, but this also shows a deficit.

At the end of 1980, the value of all frozen investment projects amounted to 821,000 million zlotys. At least four years are needed to complete the projects that have been started. In past years, the percentage of outlays for modernization, i.e., 25 percent of the total outlays for industry, was too small.

A PROGRAM FOR RESOLVING THE CRISIS:

The aims, priorities and assumptions of the economic policy:

These include introducing order and disciplined organization and technology in the economy; halting the declines in production, the national income, foreign trade turnover, the population's living standard, and market supplies; a tangible improvement in raw materials, and component supplies; activating mechanisms aimed at restoring development trends; a considerable lessening of the inflation threat, raising the value of the currency, the eventual discontinuing of food rationing; slowing down increases in foreign debt.

Introduction of economic reform in practice:

The first stage of central economic administration reform has been carried out. Draft laws on enterprises and self-government have been prepared, and some proposed solutions have already been introduced in crafts and state farms. New supply prices and new principles of annual planning should be established by January 1, 1982. The gradual reorganization of industrial amalgamations and the establishment of economic associations is another urgent task.

Directions of activity:

Halting the production decline and achieving steady growth is conditioned first of all on increasing raw material supplies. In order to boost farm production, the government will change the industrial production structure, making it possible to increase supplies of agricultural production tools and goods.

New economic and financial principles will be introduced on January 1, 1982, in order to enable private farms to finance their own development.

The industrial structure will be changed considerably. The aim is to save fuels and energy. There will be cuts in the general production level of the most energy- and material-consuming products, like steel and cement.

Increasing coal production is of paramount importance. The coal industry has been given preference for materials, machinery, and spare parts. Employment in mines will be increased.

A hard-currency import and cooperation fund will be set up in the second half of this year (1981) out of revenues gained from exports to the capitalist countries. The import of raw materials and components will continue to be centrally managed. Steps will be taken to cancel already-concluded contracts for investment goods and supplies. The production of goods for which too large an amount of imported materials and components is needed will be discontinued as of January 1, 1982.

Restoring Market Balance:

The government has concluded that price reforms are the only way to improve the market situation quickly and achieve progress in overcoming the crisis. Two variations have been proposed: the first provides for a one-time increase in the prices of basic foodstuffs, coal, gas, electric power, detergents, cosmetics, and such industrial consumer goods as high-quality radio sets, refrigerators, or luxury cars. The annual value of the increase would come to 700,000 million zlotys. It should be implemented in the second half of this year, at the latest. The cost of living would go up immediately by about 55 percent.

The second possibility foresees a gradual price hike in various groups of food articles, tobacco and cigarettes, liquors, energy, and fuels. It would take place over a period of eighteen months between July, 1981 through December, 1982. Prices of industrial consumer goods would start to go up in the first half of next year.

The government has suggested that the average monthly increase in the cost of living resulting from the price hikes be taken as the basis for the system of wage increases which would amount to 100 percent of the average rise for the lowest wage earners, 50 percent for those with average incomes, and 25 percent for people with high incomes.

Redressing the payment balance and reorienting the economy into producing goods for exports:

The rise in exports is to be promoted by: a reform of supply prices, fixing the exchange rate of the zloty in foreign trade so as to insure the profitability of exports, and using the profit earned from exports for the development of business. Free industrial capacities will be converted to producing goods for export. Polish enterprises will be allowed to set up joint companies with firms from capitalist countries. Balance of trade in sales of food and agricultural products to capitalist countries is of key importance in the coming three or four years.

Prospects for getting out of the crisis:

With average favorable external conditions, and successful implementation of the assumptions of the above program, two or three years will be necessary to attain the highest recorded level of plant production from the period before the crisis; three years in animal breeding; three or four years in industrial production; five or six years in gross national income. In six or seven years it will be possible to start reducing the foreign debt. The crisis period can be shortened: if production of coal and other raw materials is increased, if there are favorable growing conditions in agriculture, if exports are increased and the prices paid for Polish goods sold overseas increases, if economic reforms are successfully carried on, and if closer relations with socialist countries are developed.

Polish Press Agency, *Newsletter,* No. 57/442, August, 1981

Appendix F

Who Are the Anti-Socialists?

A Speech by Edward Lipinski to the Solidarity Congress

I have delivered many speeches in my life but never have I been as excited as I am today. Perhaps it is because of the conditions in which I am now taking the floor.

Where shall I begin?

The year is 1976. Polish society and the Polish nation were threatened from every side, culturally, politically, morally, socially, and economically—and this menace was increasing.

The events of 1976—the workers' riots—prompted the police and security services to beat and torture people. Masses of laborers were fired in Radom and in Ursus.

The idea was suggested that we try and defend ourselves and protect those unjustly accused. The Committee of Workers' Defense and the Committee for Social Defense were set up.

Times have changed since 1976. A great social force has emerged—*Solidarnosc*. This assembly is quite unique in the history of the last decades.

The conditions in which KOR operates have also changed. Thus, KOR has decided to cease activity because of these new conditions, and because these new forces operate more effectively than KOR could. Allow me, therefore, to read the KOR statement which, in a way, is its last will and testament. [The text of the statement appears earlier in this book.]

Despite these changes, I cannot help feeling that the struggle is not over. I was frightened when I heard Kania speak at a Party meeting of the bloodshed which threatens us. I was frightened to hear General Jaruzelski say that he is ready to mobilize the army for the defense of socialism in Poland.

What is this supposed to mean? How can the army protect socialism in Poland by shooting the people? There were two programs on TV presenting conversations with soldiers. They stated fervently that they are ready to defend socialism and to obey orders. And what order is to be given? What order will the authorities give in order to protect socialism? Shoot?

The defense of socialism is a question of principles, a question of theory, a question of political views. How can a situation arise in which the top representatives of authority threaten us with military intervention to stave off an apparent threat to socialism? In what way is socialism jeopardized in Poland? What are these anti-socialist and anti-revolutionary forces?

Socialism, as defined in the classic works of socialism, was to be a better, post-capitalist economy, with freedom broader than in capitalism, with the creation of conditions in which everyone would be given an opportunity to develop universally, to have unlimited access to the products of culture and civilization.

However, they created a socialism with a faulty economy, an incompetent economy, a wasteful economy; and it is this socialism that has led to an economic collapse unparalleled in the course of the last hundred or two hundred years. Maybe similar conditions exist in Cambodia, where the socialist system liquidated three and a half million people in defense of their socialism.

This socialism of waste, this socialism of prisons, censorship, and police, this socialism has been destroying us for thirty years, as it is now doing with some other nations.

I have considered myself a socialist since 1906. But the real struggle for a better and democratic economy, for ownership of the nonstate means of production (where a group of new nonprivate owners has come into being), this is a struggle for democratic management of the factories, for the political freedom which is supposed to be a characteristic of the socialist state, for the abolition of censorship, for the real possibility of planned development in the Polish nation.

There *are* anti-socialist and anti-revolutionary forces. But, in my opinion, it is the government's socialism that is anti-socialist and anti-revolutionary.

They threaten us with bloodshed, and under the sponsorship of the Party, they publish such papers as *Rzeczywistosc* (*Reality*), *Ekran* (*Screen*), and the organs of the branch trade unions. [The branch trade unions were the remnants of the old PUWP-controlled Central Council of Trade Unions, which was dissolved after the formation of Solidarity, and as such were hostile to Solidarity. Anti-Semitism was sometimes used by both sides, though never officially.] Anti-Semitism is growing: the papers of the branch unions are quoting the Protocols of the Elders of Zion, which are anti-state and anti-Jewish, and which had already been crated by the Okhrana before World War I.

Under the sponsorship of General Jaruzelski, they publish *Zolnierz Wolnosci* (*Soldier of Freedom*), a communist, anti-fascist paper. One of the recent issues carried an article attacking the villains from Solidarity and KOR who argue that Katyn was a crime committed by the Russians. No, the article says, it was the Germans who were responsible for Katyn. [In 1943, during World War II, the German government announced the discovery of a mass grave at Katyn, near Smolensk, containing the bodies of ten thousand Polish officers. It charged that they had been killed by the Russians during 1940. The Soviet authorities, who had captured many Polish officers during the Soviet-German partition of Poland in 1939, denied responsibility for the crime and accused the Germans. Most Poles, however, still blame the Russians.] This paper is the organ of the Polish army and is expected to shape the moral attitude of soldiers and officers.

We are not all socialists, but we are all fighting for the same goal. There are no significant forces in Poland which desire the capitalization of the means of production. There are no such forces in the Katowice Steelworks or in the Lenin Steelworks.

But everybody understands that as far as small-scale trade, small-scale industry and restaurants are concerned, these should be run by the private sector that can effectively run such establishments. To socialize them would be to bureaucratize them, to endow them with the basic attributes of a collective system which cannot adapt to changing conditions. Private property is better for the above establishments, but there are no anti-socialist and anti-revolutionary forces now that demand a capitalist takeover of heavy industry.

There *are* forces which strive after freedom, which demand freedom, which demand normal living conditions for the Polish people, but *these* are not the *real* anti-socialist forces.

[Taken from the *Congress Post*, the English-language edition of the union's daily congress news bulletin for September 29, 1981. The speech was given on September 28.]

Appendix G

The Program of ISTU Solidarity

THE FIRST NATIONAL CONFERENCE OF THE DELEGATES

Who We Are and Where We Should Go

The ISTU Solidarity was born out of the strike movement in 1980, the greatest mass movement of workers in the history of Poland. This labor movement started among the workers of the huge state enterprizes in various regions of the country, and had its historical turning point on the coast of Poland in 1980. In one year, this movement has permeated the entire working world of Poland, reaching workers and farmers, intelligentsia and artisans alike.

At the begining of our Union, there were, quite simply, only average people, men and women with their sufferings, disillusionments, needs, hopes, desires, fears, and longings. Our Union was born out of the spontaneous revolt of a segment of society which had been afflicted for more than three decades by abuse of basic citizens' and human rights, by official encouragement of ideological and economic discrimination. The Union was and is the embodiment of that protest against the existing system.

But we are not concerned solely with the material conditions of life, even though we have lived poorly, and worked hard, and often fruitlessly. History has taught us that there can be no bread without freedom. We are also concerned with justice, democracy, truth, due process of law, human dignity, freedom of conscience, and a general moral reorientation of the Republic—and not just with bread, butter, and sausage. All of these values were kept too much in disrepute for us to believe that, without their reestablishment as guiding principles for the state, anything would really change. Economic protest had to be merged simultaneously with social protest, and social protest with moral protest.

This social and moral protest did not originate overnight: There is mingled in the recent history of Poland the heritage of the blood of the Poznan workers of 1956, of the coastal workers of 1970, of the students revolting in 1968, and of the Radom and Ursus workers in 1976. This heritage includes a long series of independent actions by workers, intelligentsia, and youth, and of Church efforts to maintain human values. Our Union was born from this struggle and will remain faithful to it.

We are an organization which combines characteristics of a trade union and of a mass social movement. The combination of these characteristics strengthens our organization, and defines our role in the life of the whole nation. Thanks to the creation of a powerful union organization, Polish society has ceased to be dispersed, disorganized, and lost, and has united under the slogans of solidarity, regaining strength and hope. Conditions have been created for a genuine national rebirth. Our Union, as the largest single representative of the Polish working people, wants to be and shall be an agent of this rebirth.

ISTU Solidarity combines many different social currents. It unites people of different ideologies, political beliefs, and religious convictions, regardless of their nationality. We are united by protest against injustice, excesses of power, and the monopolization of the right to define and express the desires of the whole nation. We are united in protest against a state treating its citizens as its exclusive property; against government taking from the working people the right to be truly represented in their conflicts with the state; against the arrogance of self-appointed rulers who decide how much freedom they will give their subjects; against men who reward political obedience instead of allowing independence and initiative. We are determined to stop official lying and deception. We must cease wasting the results of the nation's hard work.

We are a force which exists not just for protest, but to rebuild a Poland suitable for everyone. We are the one single force in Poland which appeals to common human values.

At the basis of any action must be respect for man. The state exists to serve man, not to rule him. Government should serve society as a whole; it cannot do this if it is confined to a single political party. The state must be the common weal of the entire nation. Labor is senseless unless it is subordinated to man and to his genuine needs.

The basis of our national and social rebirth must be a return to a proper hierarchy of goals. Solidarity in defining its goals takes inspiration from Christian ethics, from our national tradition, and from the democratic tradition of the working world. Our new initiative for action is the recent encyclical by Pope John Paul II on human labor. Solidarity, as a mass movement of working people, is also a movement for the moral rebirth of the nation.

We consider government by the people a principle which we cannot surrender. Government by the people cannot be government by groups which put themselves above society, appropriating the right to decide the needs of society and to represent its interests. Society must be able to express the plurality of political and social ideologies. Society must have the possibility of organizing itself in such a manner that its members have a just share in the material and spiritual wellbeing of the country; the society must be able to free its potential creative forces. We want genuine socialization of the economic and governmental system. Therefore, we follow the path towards a self-governing Poland.

The idea of freedom and of full sovereignty is dear to us. With our full strength we shall support all that actually increases the sovereignty of the nation, and favors free development of national culture and the transmission of our national heritage. Our national identity must be respected fully.

Our Union, which was created and acts under so difficult conditions, is now blazing a trail. From the very beginning, the people have been coming to us, those who had in their hearts a concern for these important matters, but who had nowhere to go for understanding and support. There is, perhaps, no part of life where something is not expected of us, where the Union is not counted on by the masses for strength and for social and moral authority. But at the same time, we must still fight for our very existence, to organize at all levels, and to learn, often from our own mistakes, a proper method of action and to complete our goals.

Our program is a program of striving for the goals which we have put forward, a program in which are reflected the desires and aspirations of the entire society. Our program is also the result of those aspirations, the means through which we want to reach long-range goals by solving immediate matters at close range. This is our work, our struggle, our duty.

THE CURRENT SITUATION IN POLAND

The mass social movement known as Solidarity has changed the basic foundation of the state, making possible the development of various independent social institutions, new as well as old, which until recently were subordinated to governmental authorities, but are now free from control. The birth of organizations independent of the government should be considered as a sign of the alterations now taking place in our country. Thanks to them, society may now attempt the realization of its goals, and effectively defend its rights for the first time.

Similarly, conditions for exercising power have been altered substantially; in order to work effectively, we have taken into consideration the will of the people, and acted accordingly in compliance with the Gdansk, Szczecin, and Jastrzebiec agreements. Reform of the economy should have been implemented by the government subsequent to the signing of their agreements, along with reform of the state and its institutions. We had the right to expect such changes from the government. The present method of governing the country based on the total supremacy of central party-state institutions has led the country to ruin. Failure to make such changes over the past year, in spite of the fact that it has been impossible to govern in the old fashion, has merely increased societal chaos and hastened the possibility of economic catastrophe. No other country in Europe since the Second World War has had a peacetime economy in such dire straits as Poland's. Society has shown tremendous patience and determination, in spite of a pervasive weariness and disappointment. But there is danger that this weariness and impatience will finally change into blind rage or mass destruction, or on the other hand reduce the mass of the people into a state of impotent lethargy. We must not lose hope that there is a way out of the crisis.

In the face of our national tragedy Solidarity cannot limit itself to waiting for change, patiently exerting pressure on the authorities to fulfill their obligations from the agreements. For society we are the sole guarantor of those agreements. Therefore, our Union deems it its basic duty to undertake all possible short term actions to save our country from a fall into economic and political depression, and to rescue society from wretchedness, discouragement, and self-destruction. There is no other way to this goal but the reconstruction of the state and the economy on the basis of democracy and social initiative.

We are fully aware that Polish society expects from us the fulfillment of these goals in such a manner that people will be able to live in peace. The nation will not forgive anyone the betrayal of the ideals from which Solidarity arose. The nation will not forgive anyone whose deeds, even from the best intentions, lead to bloodshed and the destruction of our material and spiritual wealth. This awareness requires from us the gradual implementation of our ideals in such a way that each succeeding change will get the support of the people.

Our feelings of responsibility force us to notice the alignment of forces set up in Europe after the Second World War. We want to carry out the transformation started by us without violating international alliances. Under our program, such alliances may actually receive more genuine guarantees than currently. Poland is animated by deep feelings of dignity, patriotism, and its own traditions; it may be a worthy partner to other states only if it undertakes the obligations willingly and with full awareness.

Today's situation in the country has forced us to create programs for various fields. Firstly, we must implement quick actions necessary for national survival during the coming difficult winter. At the same time, the basic program of economic reforms cannot be delayed, nor can a program of social policy for the reconstruction of public life, moving towards a self-governing republic.

THESES AND CHAPTER ABBREVIATIONS

Thesis: We demand the introduction of self-government to insure democracy on all levels of management of a new socio-economic order which will combine planning, self-government, and marketing.

This section considers the Union's stand on economic reform and the crisis. The government has announced a program for stabilizing the economy, but the Union cannot support this program, because it does not employ many of the important economic reserves and because it clearly has no public support. The crisis can be overcome speedily only by authorities who enjoy full credibility. Therefore, it is necessary to appoint to the most important positions in economic planning the best experts available, particularly those who have not been already discredited. Centralized management should be abolished and the administration of the economy should be the socially-owned business managed indirectly by its workers, and run by a director appointed and dismissed by workers' councils. The struggle for economic reform must be carried out under social control. Thus, it is necessary to set up a Social Council for National Economy, which will appraise governmental economic policy, economic legislation, and the whole economic situation of Poland. This Council will have the right to forward to the *Sejm* proposals for economic legislation. Its members must have access to the mass media.

PROTECTION OF LABOR AS THE BASIC TASK OF THE UNION

Thesis: The right to work must be respected and the wage structures reformed.

Solidarity supports the universal right to work and is against unemployment. In work places threatened with staff reductions, factory commissions should consider the possibility that redundant workmen might perform some different tasks or work shorter hours at full pay.

THE SOLIDARITY SOCIETY—THE SOCIAL POLICY

Thesis: The Union wants to direct the social initiatives awakened by the protest towards the fulfillment of immediate social needs.

The Union will defend the interests of families, old people, the handicapped, and invalids. Since the biological health of the nation is now endangered, the Union will pay particular attention to national health protection. The right to adequate housing is basic; everyone should have input to establishing housing policies. Every working person should have leisure time and the opportunity to use it for participation in cultural events.

SELF-GOVERNING REPUBLIC

Thesis: Social, ideological, and cultural pluralism should be the basis of democracy in the self-governing republic.

This chapter is the Union's political declaration. We treat pluralism, the democratization of the state, and establishment of constitutional liberties, as basic guarantees that the sacrifices of the working people will not be wasted once again. We collaborate with other social movements and request political pluralism. But we are against having the governing bodies of our Union create political parties. A genuine workers' council will be at the basis of a self-governing Republic. These should be independent from the state/party system. The Republic will be governed administratively by autonomous territorial bodies freely elected. Self-governing bodies and organizations should be represented at the highest governmental level. The *Sejm* should be the supreme power in the state, with its deputies freely elected. The system must guarantee basic liberties, and must respect the principle of equality under the law for all citizens and institutions of public life. The judiciary must be independent. There should be an independent Constitutional Tribunal to decide the constitutionality of legislation. Citizens should have access to administrative documents. The organs of national security should be under social control. There must be scientific and intellectual freedom. The mass media belongs to society and must be under its control.

OUR UNION

Thesis: The members of our association have the right to express freely their opinions and wishes, and they have the right to associate for the realization of common goals.

The basis of Solidarity is democracy, which in turn is based on submission to the will of the majority, but with respect for the opinion of the minority. The best method for the realization of workers' and citizens' interests is agreement and compromise. If that fails, we must resort to protest actions.

THE NEW SOCIAL CONTRACT

Thesis: Solidarity demands a new social contract. The Independent, Self-Governing Trade Union Solidarity is the guarantor of the social agreements of 1980, and requests their immediate realization. There is no other road to the country's salvation but the realization of the constitutional principle of the sovereignty of the nation.

The Union is defining its program at a moment when the country is in great danger. It is impossible to live indefinitely under crisis conditions; we must get out of this crisis.

A resolution to the crisis must insure the survival of society during the harsh approaching months of winter. It must point a direction out of the crisis. It must as its first criterion demand the cooperation of the authorities and society.

An agreement on economic reform requires the cooperation of the authorities to change radically the present economic system. Reform should guarantee management of state enterprises by their workers under such an economic organization as will combine marketing laws with social planning.

Hundreds of agreements signed in the past by the government exist only on paper. Promises given by the authorities to working people should now be fulfilled.

An agreement on a self-governing Republic must point out the means for the democratization of public institutions, including the *Sejm*, political authorities, territorial government, and the economic, judicial, and educational institutions. The realization of this agreement will establish proper relations between citizens and their state.

The road to self-government is the only road by which Poland will become a credible partner to the other nations. The Union treats a new social agreement as indivisible.

Solidarity must first fulfill the promises it made to the country. We know that these will be accepted by society. No private interests singular or plural may be put above the country's interest. We do not think that we possess a monopoly on truth; we are ready to talk with the authorities in an honest and loyal dialogue; and to search for proper decisions which would best serve the country and fulfill the best interests of both employees and citizens. Let this broad agreement be on what is national, democratic, and human, concerning matters which will unite—not divide—us.

The ISTU Solidarity is the guarantor of the social agreements of 1980, and demands their realization. There is no other road to the country's salvation but the implementation of the constitutional principle of the sovereignty of the nation. Conference of Delegates, Gdansk, 7th day of October, 1981. (*Tygodnik Solidarnosc*, Warsaw, October 16, 1981.)

Appendix H

The Radom Declaration

The stance of the presidium of the National Commission and the regional Chairman of the Independent, Self-Governing Trade Union Solidarity.

The Presidium of the National Commission and the Chairmen of the regional boards of ISTU Solidarity present to the members of the Union for consultation, and to the National Commission for deliberation, the following position paper.

1. The party-state authorities used negotiations with the Union and the idea of a national accord to mislead society. Talks concerning the key demands of Solidarity (control of the food reserves, territorial autonomy, economic reform, due process of law, access to mass media) were fruitless. The Government surprised the Union by introducing into the *Sejm* the so-called provisional arrangement, which is aimed against the basic interests of the working people. During the negotiations, the authorities intensified anti-union repressions, of which the outstanding example was the beating of a bill-posting group in Chorzow, and an attack by the militia on the Cadet Firemen School in Warsaw. A rightful student strike has been prolonged on purpose by the authorities, and they are torpedoing attempts aimed at finding a solution to the Radom conflict. In addition, the VI Plenum of the CC of the PUWP decided to force through the *Sejm* legislation for extraordinary measures, while keeping the text of a bill on which may depend the fate of Poland secret from the nation. Talks about a national accord were utilized by the government to conceal the preparation of the attack on the union. In this situation, further negotiations on the subject of national accord are irrelevant.

2. Whether or not legislation giving the state extraordinary power will authorize the government to put civilians under military jurisdiction, forbid meetings and limit freedom of travel, or only withdraw the right to

strike, these powers can be put into effect only with the help of terrorism. Such an attempt would disable society through the use of force. Therefore, if the *Sejm* passes the bill granting such powers to the government the union will answer with a 24-hour protest strike throughout all of Poland. And if the government decides to use its extraordinary rights, the all-union branches and factory crews will immediately start a general strike.

3. The so-called provisional system for 1982 in practice continues the old system of central economic management while at the same time shifting to the production units and their staffs the material consequences of decisions which remain in the hands of the central authorities. This equates to an annihilation of reform and of already-approved bills on self-management of state enterprises. At the same time, it threatens numerous businesses with bankruptcy, losses, and lower wages. Together with the provisional arrangement, the government intends a drastic increase in prices. Society must pay for the nonexistent reforms. In accordance with the legal aims of the trade union, and using all available statuatory means, we shall defend the people from the effects of price hiking, closing of the factories, work reductions, and wage cuts.

4. The National Accord cannot depend on putting the Union into a repainted Front of National Unity, an idea toward which the government is leaning. Such adornment of the facade of an old structure with the hallmark of our union, and the consequent maintenance of a system which has ruined our country, would not help in battling our way out of the crisis, but would only eliminate the Union's credibility and independence, something which the government perhaps intends.

5. The Union shall not relinquish the following demands:

a) The retreat of the authorities from all anti-union repressions;

b) Introduction into the *Sejm* of trade union legislation in the form agreed upon with the Solidarity representatives;

c) The retreat of the government from the so-called provisional system, and introduction of economic reform based on self-government;

d) The conduct of democratic elections to the national councils on all levels (and establishment of a schedule for early elections to the Voievodship councils), and the subordination to them of the local administration. We shall not agree to a single electoral list, as was done in previous years;

e) Respect for the Union's control over the economy and especially over the food reserves; keeping such matters secret from the nation is not acceptable;

f) Giving to the Social Council of National Economy real influence on governmental decisions and control over the socio-economic policy of the state;

f) Ensuring that the Council, Solidarity, the Catholic Church, and the other centers of public opinion, have free access to radio and television.

These are minimal conditions for a national agreement which will make possible a mutual and effective struggle with the crisis. We will vote for such an agreement.

[*Tygodnik Solidarnosc*, Warsaw, December 11, 1981. The government of General Jaruzelski proclaimed martial law two days later.]

Appendix I

Members of the Presidium
of the National Commission of Solidarity

1. Lech Walesa (President), 38, electrician.
2. Ryszard Blaszczyk, 27, technician.
3. Zbigniew Bujak, 27, electromonter.
4. Wladyslaw Fraszyniuk, 27, driver.
5. Miroslaw Krupinski, 41, engineer.
6. Jacek Merkel, 27, engineer.
7. Andrzej Konarski, 29, technician.
8. Janusz Onyszkiewicz, 43, mathematician.
9. Grzegorz Palka, 31, economist.
10. Jozef Patyna, 34, technician.
11. Grazyna Przybylska-Wendt, 46, M.D.
12. Zdzislaw Rozwalik, 38, smith.
13. Waclaw Sikora, 33, technician.
14. Andrzej Slowik, 32, driver.
15. Leszek Waliszewski, 27, engineer.
16. Jan Waszkiewicz, 37, mathematician.
17. Stanislaw Wadolowski, 43, technician.
18. Antoni Tokarczuk, 30, sociologist.

Tygodnik Solidarnosc, Warsaw, October 23, 1981

Bibliography

Bethell, Nicholas. *Gomulka, His Poland, His Communism.* New York: Holt, Rinehart & Winston, 1969.

Biblioteka Pomostu. *Polski Sierpien 1980.* New York: Biblioteka Pomostu, 1981.

Constitution of the Polish People's Republic. Warsaw: Krajowa Agencja Wydawnicza, 1981.

Dusza, Edward. *Rozmowa z Mieczyslawem Gryszkiewiczem.* Stevens Point, Wisconsin: Gwiazda Polarna, 1981.

Express Wieczorny (Warsaw), June 30; July 14, 1981.

Glos Pracy (Warsaw), September 6, 1980.

Kultura (Paris), n.d. 1959; 1960 (Nos. 141, 156).

Kultura (Warsaw), September 20, 1981.

Los Angeles Times, September 19, 28, 30, 1981.

Macdonald, Oliver, ed. *The Polish August.* San Francisco: Ztangi Press, 1981.

Na Antenie (London), July, 1981.

New York Times, September 19, 1981.

Nowy Dziennik (New York), September 26-27, 1981.

Offredo, Jean. *Lech Walesa Czyli Polskie Lato.* Paris: La Cove, 1981.

Polityka (Warsaw), September 26, 1981.

Pomost (Chicago), July -September, 1981.

Protokoly Porozumien Gdansk, Szczecin, Jastrzebie. Warsaw: RSW "Prasa-Ksiazka-Ruch" 1981.

Radio Free Europe. *RAD Background Report/91 & 263.* Munich: Radio Free Europe, 1980.

Robinson, William F., ed. *August 1980, The Strikes in Poland.* Munich: Radio Free Europe, 1981.

Sztandar Mlodych (Warsaw), March 30, 1981.

Singer Daniel. *The Road to Gdansk.* New York: Monthly Review Press, 1981.

Solidarnosc (Gdansk), April 6, 1981.

Torunczyk, Barbara. *Gdansk 1980 Oczyma Swiadkow.* London: Polonia Book Fund, 1980.

Trybuna Ludu (Warsaw), August, 1980-December, 1981.

Tygodnik Solidarnosc (Warsaw), August-November, 1981.

U.S. Foreign Broadcast Information Service. *Daily Report,* August, 1980-December, 1981.

Zycie Warszawy, March 29; June 10, 11, 1981.

Biographical Notes

Babiuch, Edward: Prime Minister until September 24, 1980. Removed from the Politbureau and the Central Committee, and resigned as Prime Minister. Born in 1917. *Apparatchik*.

Borusewicz, Bogdan: Historian. Member of KOR. Co-editor of *Robotnik*. Head of propaganda in Gdansk Solidarity. Co-founder of Free Trade Union.

Bujak, Zbigniew: Born in 1954 to a peasant family. Worker and leader of Mazowsze Solidarity. One of the radicals. Presently in hiding.

Gierek, Edward: Born in 1913; raised in France. Joined French Communist Party in 1931; deported for organizing a strike. Joined Communist Party in Belgium, but returned to Poland in 1948. Politbureau 1956 and 1959. Deputy to *Sejm* 1957; First Secretary, Katowice City Party 1957-70. Leader of young Party technocrats. Replaced Gomulka as First Secretary in 1970.

Gomulka, Wladyslaw: Born in 1905. Helped establish PUWP and was Secretary of its Central Committee (1943-49). Deputy Premier 1945-49. Purged in 1949 for alleged support of Tito. Imprisoned 1951-54. Readmitted to the Party and became First Secretary in 1956. Dominated Polish politics for next fifteen years. Forced to resign December 1970 following widespread rioting; purged from Central Committee in 1971.

Grabski, Tadeusz: Born in Warsaw in 1929 to an intelligentsia family. Doctor of Economics. Career officer in the early fifties. Party and government posts. Critical of Gierek's economic policy. Critical of Kania. Chairman of a special commission to investigate former PUWP and governmental officials.

Jablonski, Henryk: Chairman of State Council. Professor of History. Member of the Polish Academy of Science. Was a member of the Polish Socialistic Party before the war. Born in 1909.

Jagielski, Mieczyslaw: Born in 1924. Graduate of the Central School of Planning. Minister of Agriculture. Deputy Prime Minister until July 1981.

Jaruzelski, Wojciech. Born in 1923. Deported with family to the Soviety Union during the last war. Chief of the Army Central Political Board 1960-65; Chief of the General Staff 1965-68; Deputy Minister of Defense 1962-68; Minister of Defense since 1968. Prime Minister. First Secretary, October 1981 to date. Full member of the Politbureau since 1971.

Kania, Stanislaw: Born in 1927 to a peasant family. Member of Communist Peasants' Battalions (partisans) during the last war. *Apparatchik* and graduate of Party's university. Was in charge of State-Church relations and the security forces. First secretary, 1980-October, 1981.

Kozlowski, Jan: Born in 1929. One of the founding members of the Independent Peasant Union in 1978. Editor of *Placowka*.

Kozlowski, Marek: Born in 1952. Locksmith. Imprisoned a number of times since 1972. Testified against militia brutality.

Lis, Bogdan: Born in 1953. Formerly a worker. First Deputy Chairman of the Solidarity Consultative Commission. Founding member of Interfactory Strike Committee in August, 1980. Member of PUWP, but dismissed from the party in October, 1981.

Lukasiewicz, Jerzy: Born in 1931 to an intelligentsia family. University graduate in Social Science. *Apparatchik*. Member of the Politbureau since 1971. Propagandist and the chief architect of Gierek's propaganda of success. In disgrace now; deprived of decorations, etc.

Moczulski, Leszek: Born in 1930. Studied law and history. Author of many books. Founding member of ROPCiO, and Confederation for Independent Poland.

Olszowski, Stefan: Born in 1931. Graduate of Lodz University in Philology. Party activist and head of a number of important departments. Secretary of CC for propaganda; controls media; considered a hardliner. Opposed Gierek's economic policy.

Pinkowski, Jozef: Born in 1929 to a working family. Graduate of School of Economy. *Apparatchik*. Prime Minister from August 24, 1980 to February 12, 1981.

Rakowski, Mieczyslaw: Born in 1926 to a peasant family. Doctor of History. Author of many books. Party activist and the editor of an important Party weekly *Polityka*. Member of CC and Deputy Prime Minister.

Walentynowicz, Anna: Born in 1929, daughter of a gardener. Worker actively engaged in Free Trade Union activities. The demand for her return to work after being fired was one of the reasons for the August strike in Gdansk. Critical of Walesa for not being enough of a radical. Connected with KOR.

Walesa, Lech: Born in 1943. Electrical worker. Active in Free Trade Unions. Became a national figure through his leadership of the Gdansk strike. Has four sons and three daughters. Interned.

Glossary

Aktiv: An "activist" in Polish political life.

Apparatchik: A career member of the Polish Communist Party; a professional governmental bureaucrat.

Armia Krajowa: The "Home Army"; a secret, underground anti-German organization active during World War II.

CC: Central Committee.

CPSU: Communist Party, Soviet Union.

CRZZ: *Centralna Rada Zwiazkow Zawodowych*; the Central Council of Trade Unions, the governing body of the official, Party-supported Polish labor movement.

"Commercial Prices"; These inflated prices (about three times those prevailing in general stores) were applied to high-quality goods offered at special commercial shops; it was the Government's deliveries to such stores (to the exclusion of the general marketplace) that started the strike movement.

Dagome Iudex: An early Polish law promulgated by King Mieszko I, the first Polish monarch to accept Christianity; his acceptance of Rome's protection assured Poland's continuing adherence to Catholicism over Eastern Orthodoxy.

"Duality of Power": The polarization of Polish politics between the official Government and opposition elements.

Finlandization: A suggested solution to the Polish crisis, in which Poland, like Finland, would gain semi-independence under freely-elected governments, but still fall under massive Russian influence.

GUKPPiW: *Glowny Urzad Kontroli Prasy, Publikacji i Widowisk*; Central Office for the Control of Press, Publications, and Public Performances. The official Government censorship office.

Gdansk Accord: *Protokoly Porozumien Gdansk, Szczecin, Jastrzebie.* The precedent-setting agreement between the striking Solidarity workers and the Government in 1980; for the text of the Accord, see Appendix C.

ISC: The Inter-Factory Strike Committee; *Miedzyzakladwy Komitet Strajkowy* (MKS), a workers' group organized to coordinate strike actions against the Government.

ISTU: Independent, Self-Governing Trade Unions; *Niezalezne Samorzadne Zwiazki Zawodowe* (NSZZ). Solidarity adopted this name rather than the term "free unions" to avoid a label that would be unacceptable to the authorities; it is phonetically close to NSZ, the National Armed Forces, an underground, anti-Communist group operating in Poland during World War II.

KOR: *Komitet Obrony Robotnikow*; Workers Defense Committee. This group of intellectuals was formed as an information center for those united in opposition to Party rule; it was dissolved in 1981 just prior to the military coup.

KPN: *Konfedaracja Polski Niepodleglej*; Confederation for an Independent Poland. An underground, illegal political opposition party, which, among other things, published clandestine books and magazines exposing Government crackdowns and atrocities. Also called the League for an Independent Poland.

KPW: See NCC.

KSS-KOR: *Komitet Samoobrony Spolecznej*; the Social Self-Defense Committee, an arm of the KOR.

Liberum Veto: The ancient right of monarchist Poland whereby any member of the *Sejm* could veto any motion brought before that body; the result of this principle was a virtual paralyzation of the monarchy to the benefit of the noble classes, and the ultimate destruction of the weak Polish state.

MDHR: Movement for the Defense of Human and Citizen Rights; *Ruch Obrony Praw Czlowieka i Obywatela* (ROPCiO). A semi-legal opposition group comprised mainly of intellectuals.

MKS: See ISC.

MO: *Milicja Obywatelska*; Citizens' Militia. The official Polish police force.

NCC: National Coordinating Commission; *Krajowa Komisja Porozumiewawcza* (KPW).

National Unity Front: *Front Jednosci Narodowej*. An official coalition of supposedly non-Communist and Communist parties, formed after World War II when the Communists took power; the "independent" parties included in the Front are Government-run and -supported. Members include the PUWP, PZSL, and the Social Democrats.

Natolin Group: A loose coalition of hardline Stalinist members of the Party during the 1956 Polish crisis.

Nomenklatura: The Party rules whereby only Party members may obtain certain choice jobs or benefits; in general, the higher the rank of the Party member, the choicer the job he or she may obtain.

ORMO: The Voluntary Reserve of Citizens' Militia.

October Revolution (1956): The first internal Polish upheaval under Communist rule, an event which toppled the Government, and set the pattern for later actions by the people. The riots were prompted primarily by economic considerations.

Odnowa: A Polish word meaning "renewal" or "reformation," used to describe the changes, both political and social, which have come about since 1980 as a result of the Solidarity movement.

PPR: Polish People's Republic. The official designation of the Polish state.

PSL: *Polskie Stronnictwo Ludowe*; the Polish Peasants Party. A leading political party of Poland before and during World War II (the leaders of the PSL spent much of the war in British exile), the Peasant's Party was subsumed by the Communists in 1947-48, at which time its name was changed to the PZSL (see below).

PUWP: Polish United Workers Party; *Polska Zjednoczona Partia Robotnicza* (PZPR). The official name of the Polish Communist Party.

PZPR: See PUWP.

PZSL: *Polskie Zjednoczone Stronnictwo Ludowe*; Polish United Peasants Party. This successor to the Polish Peasants Party is Government-run and -supported, and completely follows the Party line.

Plenum: An official meeting of the leadership of a Polish governmental body.

"Polish Strikes": A system of labor opposition formulated after World War I in Poland, whereby the workers occupy their factories until they reach a settlement. Communist leader Wladyslaw Gomulka participated in several of these early strike actions. The technique was also used by Solidarity.

"Provisory Arrangement": *Prowizorium Systemowe*. An agreement whereby the existing Governmental and social structures would be maintained until both sides of the conflict could agree on a new system.

ROPCiO: See MDHR.

Radom Declaration: A Union document criticizing Parliamentary legislation "contrary to the interests of the working people"; it became the official position of Solidarity.

"Radomgate": Clandestine tapes of a secret Solidarity meeting, at which leaders of the organization talked about the overthrow of the Government; the tapes were widely publicized and transcribed by the official Government press.

Rady Wojewodzkie: The regional governing councils of the Voievodships, roughly equivalent to state legislatures or county boards in the United States.

Robotnik: *The Worker*. An underground labor journal.

Ruch: A political movement; also the name of an official Polish publisher.

SB: *Sluzba Bezpieczenstwa*; the secret police.

Samisdat: Self-published (often typed) underground books and magazines, usually anti-Government in nature.

Sejm: Diet or Parliament; the official Polish national governing body.

Solidarity: *Solidarnosc*. The leading independent, self-governing trade union, now officially suspended under martial law [see also Appendices D and G].

Taternik or *Taternicy* (plural): Students who smuggle books printed in the West through Czechoslovakia into Poland; the word derives from the Tatra Mountains.

Trybuna Ludu: *People's Tribune*. The Party's official daily newspaper.

Tygodnik Solidarnosc: Solidarity's official weekly newspaper, now suspended.

Voievod: *Wojewoda*. The chief administrator of a Voievodship. Roughly equivalent to a state governor or county mayor in the United States.

Voievodship: *Wojewodztwo*. The regional Polish administrative unit, roughly equivalent to a small state or county in the United States.

WRON: *Wojskowa Rada Ocalenia Narodowego*; the Military Council of National Salvation. The group set up by Jaruzelski to run the martial-law government, thereby bypassing the official Governmental structures already in place.

Warsaw Pact: A series of treaties binding the Soviet Union with its Eastern Bloc satellites, including provisions for mutual defense.

ZBoWiD: *Zwiazek Bojownikow o Wolnosc i Demokracje*; the Union of Fighters for Freedom and Democracy. The official Government veterans' organization.

ZMP: *Zwiazek Mlodziezy Polskiej*; Union of Polish Youth. The young communists league, superseded by ZMS circa 1957.

ZMS: *Zwiazek Mlodziezy Socjalistycznej*; Union of Socialist Youth. The official young communists organization.

Zloty: The official Polish monetary unit, worth about 1.3 American cents at the official exchange rate, but much less at the black market rate.

Znak: "Sign." A semi-formal group of Catholic members of the *Sejm*.

Zolnierz Wolnosci: *Soldier of Freedom*. The official Polish Army newspaper.

Zycie Warszawy: *Life of Warsaw*. The Warsaw daily newspaper, indirectly influenced by the Government, but not an official publication.

Index

PZPR), 12, 19, 35-36, 40, 44, 46, 53, 61-62, 74, 80, 92-93, 108, 116, 124; Plenums, 16, 24, 30, 32, 34-36, 38, 46, 52, 63-64, 124; Extraordinary Congress, 34, 36-38, 42, 47; Warning, 47
Polish Work Code, 30
Politbureau, 15, 47, 65
Polityka, 29
Porebski, Tadeusz, 37
Poznan, 10, 30, 63-66, 110
Press, Illegal, 85
Provisory Arrangement, 56, 116-117, 124
Przybylski, Jozef, 16, 92
Przybylska-Wendt, Grazyna, 118
Pulaski, Kazimierz, 14
Pyjas, Stanislaw, 81, 89
Pyka, Tadeusz, Dep. Prime Minister, 15-16, 37

Radkiewicz, Stanislaw, 23
Radom, 11
Radom Declaration, 51, 56-57, 124; Text, 116-117
Radomgate, 55, 57, 124
Radosz, Stanislaw, 23
Rakowski, Mieczyslaw, 29, 32, 36, 45, 52, 121
Reagan, Ronald, 6
Ribbentrop-Molotov Pact, 61
Robotnik, 11-12, 70, 83, 90, 120, 124
Rokossovskii, Konstantin, 64, 66, 68
Romkowski, Roman, 62
Rozwalik, Zdzislaw, 118
Rulewski, Jan, 30-31, 33, 49, 51, 55-57, 73

SB (Secret Police), 83-84, 97, 124
Salmonowicz, Stanislaw, 81
Sapelo, Jan, 28
Security Forces, 13, 19
Sejm (Diet), 41-42, 47-48, 55, 57, 71, 73-74, 94, 113-114, 116-117, 124
Sienkiewicz, Henryk, 14
Sikora, Waclaw, 118
Sikorski, Jerzy, 16, 92
Sikorski, Wladyslaw, 34
Sila Nowicki, Wladyslaw, 32, 57
Siwak, Albin, 37
Slowik, Andrzej, 118
Smiech, Romuald, 81
Sobieszek, Lech, 16
Sokolowski, Antoni, 70
Solidarity, 9+, 124
Spychalski, Marian, 64
Stalin and Stalinism, 10, 61-62, 66-68
Stanny, Tadeusz, 16, 92

Sulecki, Wladyslaw, 70
Switon, Kazimierz, 20, 70
Szczepanski, Jan, 20
Szczepanski, Maciej, 16, 23, 26
Szlachcic, Franciszek, 38
Szpakowski, Maria, 81
Szydlak, Jan, 16, 37
Szymanski, Leszek, 6, 63, 65
Szymborski, Krzysztof, 81

Taternicy, 81, 124
Tejkowski, Bernard, 80
Tokarczuk, Antoni, 118
Tri-Cities, 13
Trybuna Ludu, 14, 31, 37-39, 74, 124
Tworkowska, Maria, 81
Tygodnik Solidarnosc, 31, 39, 41, 44, 47, 50-51, 54, 56, 115, 117, 124
Tyranski, Kazimierz, 23

Ursus Tractor Factory, 11

Veterans League—See ZBoWiD

Wadolowski, Stanislaw, 52, 118
Walentynowicz, Anna, 9, 12-13, 16, 33, 88, 92, 121
Walesa, Lech, Chairman of Solidarity, 13, 15-16, 19, 22-25, 27, 29, 31-32, 48, 52, 54, 62, 68-71, 73-74, 88-90, 92, 121; at Gdansk, 9; Talks to Jagiel-ski, 18; Bydgoszcz, 33; Solidarity Conference 43, 49; Chairman, 51, 118; Tripartite talks, 53; Radomgate Tapes, 55; Last Public Statement Before Internment, 57
Waliszewski, Leszek, 118
Wankowicz, Melchior, 81
Warsaw Pact, 31, 51, 64, 75, 124
Waszkiewicz, Jan, 118
Wisniewski, Florian, 16, 92
Wojtyla, Karol—See John Paul II, Pope
Workers Guard, 14
Wrzaszczyk, Tadeusz, 16
Wyszkowski, Krzysztof, 70
Wyszynski, Stefan, Card., 14, 34, 62-63

ZBoWiD (Union of Fighters for Freedom and Democracy), 27, 124
ZMP (Polish Youth Organization), 61
ZMS (Socialist Youth Organization), 80
Zabinski, Andrzej, 20
Zabinski, Tadeusz, 37
Zablocki, Janusz, 20
Zadrozynski, Edmund, 17, 95
Zandarowski, Zdzislaw, 16, 37
Zielinski, Zbigniew, 92